RON DEMBO

&

DANIEL STOFFMAN

UPSIDE

SIMPLE RULES *of* RISK MANAGEMENT

DOWNSIDE

for the

SMART INVESTOR

doubleday canada

Doubleday Canada and colophon are trademarks.

Library and Archives Canada Cataloguing in Publication

Dembo, Ron S
Upside, downside : simple rules of risk management for the
smart investor / Ron Dembo,
Daniel Stoffman.

Includes index.

ISBN-13: 978- 0-385-66159-1
ISBN-10: 0-385-66159-2

1. Investments. 2. Risk management. 3. Finance, Personal.
I. Stoffman, Daniel II. Title.

HG4521.D453 2006   332.67′8   C2005-906400-5

Jacket and text design: Kelly Hill
Printed and bound in the USA

Published in Canada by
Doubleday Canada, a division of
Random House of Canada Limited

Visit Random House of Canada Limited's website: www.randomhouse.ca

BVG   10   9   8   7   6   5   4   3   2   1

Ron Dembo would like to dedicate
this book to his two daughters,
Justine and Ella,
for giving him tremendous
Upside with little Downside.

CONTENTS

one

the THREE RULES *of* RISK

IN 2004, Anthony Richards of London, England, liquidated all his possessions and went to Las Vegas with the proceeds—$135,000, all he had in the world except for the clothes he was wearing. After trading the money in for chips at the Plaza Hotel casino and playing some low-stakes games to warm up, he strode to a roulette table and bet it all on red.

The ball landed on Red 7 and Richards doubled his money. Unlike most big winners, he knew enough to quit while he was ahead. He arrived back in London twice as rich as when he had left.

All of us take risks every day of our lives. When we walk down the sidewalk we ignore the risk that a big truck will go out of control and mow us down. We know this might happen, but the odds are low, so we bet against it. The upside of being able to use the sidewalk offsets the downside of the small likelihood that we might be injured or killed.

To put it another way, most of the risks we take each day are calculated risks. Whether consciously or instinctively, we analyze various future scenarios before we act, to ensure that the odds are in our favour.

Except in our financial lives. Even though our financial security is crucial to our well-being, both present and future, we take risks with our money that we would never take with our personal safety. Often without realizing it, we do the financial equivalent of dashing out into a busy street and into the face of fast-moving traffic.

Obviously, Anthony Richards (not his real name) was taking a wild gamble. But many other people, who consider themselves cautious and responsible and who would never dream of doing what Richards did, also take unreasonable risks with their money, often unknowingly. Take the case, reported in *The New York Times,* of George Casterline, a longtime employee of Corning Inc., of Corning, N.Y. When, in the 1990s, the value of the Corning stock he owned reached $500,000, he began planning for an early retirement. Then the telecommunications companies that were customers for Corning's fibre-optic cables suffered severe setbacks. Corning stock went into freefall, dropping from $113 to just over $1, and Casterline had to put his retirement plans on hold.

Thousands of employees like Casterline have taken advantage of plans that encourage workers to buy stock in the companies they work for. Few of them would consider themselves reckless gamblers. But in fact, their financial situations are almost as risky as was that of Anthony Richards when he walked up to the Las Vegas roulette table with his life savings in hand.

What if Casterline, when his Corning holdings hit $500,000, had realistically assessed future scenarios? Here he was with a fortune in the stock of the same company where his human capital (his job) resided. Moreover, this company was dependent on the fate of the volatile telecommunications industry. Was the stock more likely to continue its heady ascent or to fall? Moreover, regardless of the prospects for the stock, was it wise to have one's entire financial well-being riding on the welfare of just one company, even though that company had been successful in the past? Clearly not. Any objective analysis would have quickly revealed that Casterline's downside risk was greater than the upside. If he had analyzed his situation in those terms, he could have traded in his Corning stock for a diversified portfolio and continued planning for early retirement.

As for Anthony Richards, his upside was a chance of doubling his money. Instead of $135,000, he would have $270,000. That is a respectable amount but it is not a great fortune, certainly not enough for a thirty-two-year-old to retire on. Not enough, in fact, to change Richards's life in any significant way. His downside was the strong likelihood of being left penniless. Viewed objectively, the downside vastly outweighed the upside.

But Richards didn't see it that way, an illustration of the importance that individual psychology plays in investment decisions. An older person who had lived through trying economic circumstances and struggled to accumulate a modest nest egg would not have done what Richards did. But for a young person who has never known hard times and who doesn't foresee much difficulty in starting over should he lose, the extra $135,000 he will get if he wins is worth more than the regret he will experience if he loses. In other words, in Richards's case, the upside of his Las Vegas escapade was worth more than the downside.

Traditional risk-return analysis cannot account for such seemingly perverse behaviour. Only when we understand that each investor is different and that the perception of upside and downside varies according to one's experience, age, and personality can we understand it. Each of us has to take into account our own individual situation—both financial and psychological—when we make investment decisions.

Nobody can predict the future. That is a basic fact of life, but one that seems to elude many investment advisors, managers, and financial gurus. The financial pages of our newspapers are full of predictions, most of which turn out to be wrong. For example, all forty-three forecasts by major institutions for economic growth in Britain in 1999 turned out to be wrong. Yet forecasters continue to forecast, and many otherwise rational people continue to take their forecasts seriously.

As John Kay explained in the *Financial Times,* there is a steady supply of forecasts "because there is demand: investors and businesses that continue to believe, despite the evidence, that these people really see the future in their crystal balls. Hope continues to triumph over experience, just as it does among the customers of medical quacks and racing tipsters."

We cannot predict the future because the future is inherently uncertain. The scenario planner recognizes that the future could unfold in many different ways; meanwhile, the forecaster ignores this basic fact of life. The scenario planner envisions a wide range of possible futures. Once he has assessed all the potential outcomes, he can adjust his investment portfolio accordingly—not to make it risk free, but to make it better able to maintain its value. At first glance, doing this might seem like simple common sense. And it *is* common sense—but almost nobody does it. Most investors pay more attention to the past than the future. They assume that if Corning stock went up in the past, it will also go up in the future. Rather than assessing a variety of future scenarios, they make a forecast based on one scenario: that future performance will be similar to past performance.

Not only do individuals do this, but countries and corporations do it as well. They do it despite plentiful evidence that, in the world of investment, past performance is more often than not a poor guide to the future. Many studies have demonstrated that the past performance of investment managers and mutual funds bears little or no relationship to future performance.

Regulators now require most major financial institutions to implement systems that allow them to understand their overall risk and to arrange the capital supporting their portfolios in such a way that only very extreme conditions could be devastating. It's time that individual investors did the same.

Never before has risk management been so important for the individual investor. That's because the dominant population cohort in North America, the baby boom, is approaching retirement. Its future well-being depends on the billions of dollars it has collectively invested in real estate, stocks, bonds, cash deposits, and other forms of wealth. The boomers' prosperity requires that they safeguard this wealth.

Many of them have entrusted their savings to mutual funds, assuming that the combination of professional management and diversification that funds provide is the best way to minimize risk. Yet a growing number of investors are, rightly, questioning this strategy. The fund industry has been under investigation for trading practices that favour large clients at the expense of ordinary investors. Even before these revelations, many investors were questioning their reliance on funds because funds consistently underperform the overall stock market and because their inflated fees eat away at investors' returns.

As the boomers approach retirement, they will have the time and motivation to become more actively involved in running their own portfolios. They may wish to invest directly in stocks, bonds, or exchange-traded funds (ETFs), a low-cost alternative to mutual funds. But the investor who manages his or her own portfolio needs to understand financial risk and must know how to manage it.

It is important to distinguish between taking risk and managing it. Many entrepreneurs are big risk takers, but they manage their risk well. A key aspect of managing risk, and a necessary first step, is to know what risks you are taking.

Managing risk does not mean putting everything into the relative safety of a bank deposit or government bond. That strategy is risky too because the investor runs the danger of missing out on economic growth or simply being left behind by inflation. So, our risk includes not just how much we might lose but also how much we might have made. Some retirees in the 1970s probably thought they were being cautious when they sold their houses, banked the proceeds, and moved into rental accommodation. They missed out on one of the greatest real estate booms of all time and wound up much poorer than their contemporaries who stayed invested in real estate.

In the final chapter, we will look at some advanced methods for managing financial risk. Some of these involve the use of derivatives, which are financial instruments whose value depends on the performance of an underlying security or asset. As we shall see, derivatives are valuable tools for managing risk. They are to investment portfolios what insurance is to houses.

As investors, we must accept that we live in an unstable, and therefore risky, world. Natural catastrophes and political upheavals are unpredictable yet, at the same time, virtual certainties. Our investments are affected by them and by a thousand and one other unpredictable certainties. We know that the price of oil will fluctuate, as will the major world currencies. We know that new technologies, some of them with revolutionary impacts, will appear. We know that companies will collapse and governments will fall. We know terrorists will strike.

Any of these events might have major impacts on our investments but we don't know when they will occur. So, what do we do? We think hard about the scenarios we want to consider and the ones we want to bet against and design our portfolio in such a fashion that no single event that we have chosen to consider will have a disastrous impact on it. We then make sure that we select a portfolio with more upside than downside.

Perhaps you manage your investments yourself and are looking for a more reasoned and comprehensive way to assess the future than is provided by the latest pronouncement by an investment guru. Or maybe you have put your holdings in the hands of an investment advisor. At the very least, the book will give you pertinent questions to ask your advisor the next time you meet. It will also give you a much deeper understanding of what you have in your investment portfolio because the first rule of risk is *Know What You Own*. This isn't always as simple as it may seem. For example, as of November 2002, a major Canadian mutual fund, the AIC American Focused Fund, was 93 percent invested in cash. The manager, Larry Sarbit, couldn't find any U.S. stocks he wanted to buy at then-current prices. This in no way violated any regulations and may well have been a wise strategy. When we buy a mutual fund we are paying for expert management and ought not to complain when the manager uses his expertise as he sees fit. The only problem with Sarbit's strategy was that mutual funds are advertised and sold as investment "products" of specific types. So if you own an energy fund, you have been assured your money will be invested in energy stocks. And if you want your money held in cash at a higher interest rate than your bank account pays, you would put it into a money market fund, not a U.S. equity fund. An investor who, logically, assumed she was owning a chunk of American business when she bought the AIC American Focused Fund did not know what she owned.

Rule number two is *Use Multiple Scenarios, Not Forecasts*. An investor basing his strategy on a forecast is like a roulette player gambling that the red numbers will always win. But in the real world, sometimes red wins and sometimes black wins.

A forecaster states: "X will happen." In contrast, a user of scenarios says, "X *might* happen, but so might Y and Z." In this way, scenarios encourage us to incorporate contrarian thinking. That is good, because contrarian thinking often turns out to be right. In 2000, for example, conventional wisdom held that Internet stocks would continue to rise in value. The opposite, then minority, opinion, turned out to be the correct one—to the great distress of many investors who were heavily exposed to technology stocks. Scenario planning automatically gives us the diversification we need because it forces us to ask the question, "Will any one possible scenario badly damage the value of my portfolio?"

Former U.S. Treasury Secretary Robert Rubin has a keen sense of the dangers of not thinking in terms of scenarios. "The list of firms and individuals who have gone broke by failing to focus on remote risks is a long one," he writes in his book *In an Uncertain World*.

As an example of his own scenario thinking, Rubin recalls an incident that occurred when he headed the investment firm Goldman Sachs. Jon

Corzine, head of the firm's fixed-income activities, wanted to take a large position in farm credit bonds backed by an agency of the U.S. government.

Rubin asked, "What if a problem developed in farm credit and, as extremely unlikely as it might be, the government declines to stand by its so-called moral obligation?"

"That's silly," replied Corzine, and Rubin concedes he was probably right. Nevertheless, Rubin didn't want Goldman Sachs to collapse "because something that we agreed was virtually inconceivable actually happened. In theory, you don't ever want to be in a position where even a remote risk can hurt you beyond a certain point—and you have to decide what that point is. Too often, risks that seem remote are treated as essentially nonexistent. In this case, the remote contingency never occurred, but the decision to limit the risk was right."

At the same time, Rubin admits it is impossible to be an investor and insure yourself against all remote scenarios. You have to accept *some* risks. "But even if you can't avoid all distant risks in practice," he writes, "it's sensible to think explicitly about which ones you're choosing to take and which should be diminished or avoided."

In deciding to take steps to offset the risk of the company's large position in farm credit bonds, Rubin was anticipating how much regret he would feel if the venerable firm went bankrupt because he had let it become overexposed to one investment. He was following rule number three, which is *Anticipate Regret.* This means analyzing each investment in terms of potential "regret" if things go wrong. Suppose, for example, that a broker is urging you to invest $100,000 in a stock. There are two alternatives in this case, each one involving possible regret. If you buy the stock, and the company goes broke, you could lose $100,000. But if you don't buy it, you could lose much more. It might go up ten times in value and you will have missed out on a chance to make $900,000.

Which entails the most regret? That depends on the investor. If you are rich, the loss of $100,000 may not be so serious. In that case, not buying could result in more regret than buying. But if you are not rich, $100,000 is an important part of your net worth. Losing it would entail greater regret than missing out on a windfall profit.

In other words, either decision could be wrong. The question is, which could be more wrong? Which is the riskier decision? The answer is simple: the one that could lead you to more regret. This is a more sophisticated and thorough way to assess a potential investment than the usual method of analysis—which often amounts to little more than, "I think that mutual fund will probably go up because it went up for the last three years."

Envisioning future regret automatically takes into account our overall financial situation, our personal risk tolerance, and our long-term goals each time we make an investment decision. This is different from conventional methods of risk analysis in which the risk of an investment is analyzed no differently whether the investor is a multimillionaire or an average person saving for retirement. Yet a realistic assessment of risk is not possible without taking into account the financial status, goals, and psychological makeup of the investor.

Yet another important way in which this book differs from other writings on risk is that it's written in plain English. Anyone can understand scenarios; on the other hand, you have to be a mathematician to understand such conventional risk-analysis methods as standard deviation, which is defined as follows:
$$\text{StdDev}(r) = [1/n * (r_i - r_{ave})^2]^{1/2}$$

There will be no mathematical formulas to master in the pages that follow. Instead, there will be a good deal of straightforward common sense as we explore the three rules of risk in more detail. When we have finished, you won't be able to risk-proof your investment portfolio, but you will be using "scenario thinking" and will know the right questions to ask.

You will also be able to select portfolios that have a bias toward success. You will be managing risk in a way that is both logical and consistent. In fact, you will be able to take more risks because you will know how to manage risk appropriately. You will be much better placed than an investor who does not know how to manage risk to preserve and enhance the wealth you have accumulated. Your upside will be greater than your downside. In an unpredictable world, that's the best anyone can do.

THE BOTTOM LINE

The successful investor knows how to manage risk. That means making sure that the upside of an investment portfolio is greater than the downside. This can be achieved by following three simple rules:

1. *Know What You Own*: You can't manage your risk without a deep understanding of what exactly your portfolio contains and what risks it exposes you to.

2. *Use Multiple Scenarios, Not Forecasts*: Forecasts attempt to predict the future. But the future is unknowable, which is why forecasts are usually wrong. The risk-savvy investor uses scenarios instead of forecasts. Scenarios allow us to prepare for a variety of possible futures rather than just one.

3. *Anticipate Regret*: Before buying an investment, try to imagine how much regret you might experience should the investment fail. In this way, you incorporate your own individual financial situation and risk tolerance into the decision-making process.

two

KNOW WHAT YOU OWN

SUPPOSE YOU have a car with a blank dashboard. No speedometer, no fuel gauge, no temperature gauge. You are driving down the highway. You know there is fuel in the tank because the car is still moving. But that's all you know. You don't know how much fuel you have or how long it will last. You don't know how fast you're going. You don't know if the engine is running properly or whether it's overheating.

You are in the same situation as the typical investor. He has no idea what might happen to his investments in the future as our infinitely change-able world transforms itself with every minute that passes. How would they behave, for example, if the

U.S. dollar fell by 20 percent or the price of oil tripled or a terrorist attack even worse than that of September 11, 2001, occurred?

The driver doesn't need to know the technical details of what is going on under the hood of the car. But he does need to know if the engine is too hot or if the gas tank needs to be refilled, because having knowledge of these risks allows him to take action to protect himself against them. The gauges on his dashboard give the driver just what he needs. The investor needs the same thing on his monthly investment report, but he doesn't have it. Because he doesn't have it, he doesn't really know what he owns in his investment portfolio.

At first glance, knowing what you own seems simple. Why should knowing what's in your investment portfolio be any harder than knowing what's in your garage? For the garage, it would only take a few minutes to come up with a list that might look something like this: two cars, a ladder, a lawn mower, a set of golf clubs, a half-used tin of paint, three pairs of skis, a bicycle, and a broken skateboard.

As for your financial assets and debits, a list of these might contain a few stocks, a government bond, a mutual fund, an insurance policy, a mortgage, along with a chequing account and line of credit from the bank.

Both the garage list and the financial list are lists of "things." But there is a crucial difference that makes knowing what financial goods you own much trickier than knowing what other goods you own: financial "things" are in a state of constant flux.

A lawn mower will be the same today as it will tomorrow. It will not morph from a push mower into an electric one, or from a basic model to a fully loaded one. But the stock, bond, or mutual fund will be different tomorrow. You may have purchased 100 shares of Nortel at $100 apiece. Nortel was a stock-market darling when you bought those shares. Now it's a stock-market dog and a plaything for day traders. The shares are worth a fraction of what you paid for them. But you are keeping them because you think Nortel's fortunes might revive and its shares might go up in value again. You're right: they *might*. Nobody can predict what will happen to a stock from one day to the next.

That point must be emphasized: nobody knows what will happen to financial goods in the future, and relying on the advice of those who claim to know can be fatal to one's financial health. Over a period of seven years, writer John Dorfman tracked the results of the stocks that Wall Street brokerage analysts favoured the most. These analysts are well-trained experts who do nothing but follow the fortunes of public companies. Presumably, they know more about stocks than anyone. Yet the average return of their favourites over those seven years was a loss of 5.1 percent. For the stocks these geniuses disliked, the average return was a gain of 4.6 percent.

Your difficulty in knowing what you own is especially pronounced if you own units of a mutual fund, the most popular investment vehicle of our times. A mutual fund contains dozens, sometimes hundreds, of stocks and may also include a fixed-income component of bonds and other debt instruments. The composition of the fund changes from day to day, as do the values of the various securities in it. The fund investor can't possibly know what is actually in the fund at any given moment and doesn't really need to. What she does need to know is how the various risk factors will affect her investment. For example, what is the likely impact on the fund of every one-percent change in the six-month interest rate? Or the value of the Canadian dollar, or the technology index?

Investors rarely if ever receive this information, although modern risk-management technology would make it possible for investment dealers to provide it if they wanted to. It's understandable that they don't. Risk is difficult to calculate and requires expenditures in technology that investment companies would prefer to avoid. Also, many financial advisors don't think it's necessary. But it is—as necessary as knowing whether the road you are driving on has a sharp curve ahead.

Knowing what you own, therefore, means more than just being able to define and understand investment vehicles such as mutual funds, hedge funds, and income trusts, although such knowledge is critically important. Knowing what you own also means knowing your risk. (We also need to know how to manage our risk, a subject that will be explored in the final chapter.) Suppose you sign a deal to buy a house, but the transaction does not close until six months in the future. Your problem is that banks do not guarantee a mortgage rate six months ahead. Typically, the farthest ahead a home buyer can lock in a rate is three months. So you, as party to a purchase agreement with a six-month closing, do not know what your monthly payment is going to be. You are exposed to unpredictable future fluctuations in the interest rate.

Your banker will assure you it is unlikely rates will leap so high as to cause you any serious problem. But rates have made sudden sharp moves in the past and could again. In this typical house deal, you need to understand that you own two things: a forward contract to buy a house in six months at a predetermined price and exposure to interest rates six months in the future. That exposure is not a trivial matter; before you made the deal you calculated what your monthly payment would be, based on prevailing rates. If the interest rate shoots up sharply, you might have to walk away from the deal.

Few investors assess their risk in such explicit terms. Our hypothetical home buyer may or may not take steps to leave herself less exposed to the vagaries of the interest rate in this case, but whether she does or not she is better off being aware of the risk she faces than being oblivious to it by relying on the self-interested views of her mortgage lender. While the bank is content to leave you unprotected, it makes sure its own position is protected by hedging against unexpected changes in the interest rate.

As individuals, we too should be able to protect ourselves against financial risk. Fortunately, this is already starting to happen. And as people become more aware of the availability of such risk-management tools, and more investors demand them, the financial industry will make them more widely available.

Until then, most individual investors are in the same unprotected position as major banks were thirty years ago. Until then, banking had been a simple business: a loan was a loan and a mortgage was a mortgage. The people who were running banks in the 1980s had risen through the ranks in the post–World War II era. Their idea of understanding risk consisted of analyzing the balance sheets and creditworthiness of their loan customers.

Then derivatives came along and created a whole new level of complexity. Suppose that you have a business in Canada, but most of your customers are in the U.S. You use derivatives called forward exchange-rate contracts to lock in the price you pay for U.S. dollars—that way you can run your business with some certainty about the future. The advent of computer technology made the development of individualized derivative products possible at the same time that business embarked on a rapid course of globalization and financial officers became increasingly sophisticated. These factors created demand for derivatives.

So, the banks got into the derivatives business. This was a profitable new business, but it exposed the banks to risks that traditional bankers did not know how to manage. One of the more dramatic results of this situation was the collapse in 1995 of Barings, Britain's oldest merchant bank, because of $1.4 billion in losses incurred by the derivatives trading of one rogue employee. The bank's senior managers had no tools to measure what was going on. They did not understand the risks to which the bank had been exposed. Barings Bank did not know what it owned.

Today, all major banks use risk-management systems that allow them to track their risk positions right up to the moment, twenty-four hours a day. These systems don't allow a bank to predict the future, because the future is not predictable. But they do signal when a position becomes dangerous, thereby allowing management to take corrective measures to reduce the risk exposure. To return to the automotive analogy, banks are now "driving" their portfolios with the assistance of key dashboard gauges. It's time individuals had the same gauges at their disposal. The sophisticated investor needs to make the same transition that banks have already made—from being oblivious to risk, to being aware of it, to managing it.

As risk-management technology progresses and becomes more widespread, investors will become better informed about what they own in their financial portfolios. That knowledge, in turn, will enable them to manage their risk effectively. Until then, we must make do with what information is available. And we must learn to grapple with the constant flux of the financial instruments we own.

A car also changes in value over time. If it's a very special car, it might even increase in value. But usually it will depreciate, and that depreciation is predictable. Changes in the value of financial instruments are not predictable. Moreover, financial instruments, unlike most cars, are as likely to go up in value as to decline. Sometimes financial instruments morph for no apparent reason. Other times, they change in response to economic or political events. For example, the central bank may decide to raise the interest rate. If you hold bonds, that decision will change their value. A bond, which is a loan an investor makes to a government or a corporation, might seem like an exception to the rule of unpredictability because we know for sure that a $10,000 bond will be worth $10,000 when it matures, unless the issuer goes broke and defaults on its obligations. Such calamities do happen—major countries such as Argentina and major companies such as Confederation Life have defaulted on their debt. In fact, Confederation Life went from having the highest possible credit rating to bankruptcy in six months. The financial problems of General Motors, the world's largest carmaker, led in 2005 to its debt being relegated to the status of junk bonds, meaning they had morphed from rock-solid investments to shaky ones.

Even if the issuer remains prosperous, the value of a bond, in the interval between its issue and maturity date, fluctuates just like a stock's and there is no way of knowing whether it will be worth $10,000—or more, or less—if we have to sell it before it matures.

Today, you may purchase a bond that is worth $10,000. In six months, when the semi-annual interest payment arrives in your account, you own a bond worth $10,000 plus $200. And the week after that, when interest rates rise, the market value of your bond declines. Now you own a bond worth $9,500.

When rates go up, the value of a bond goes down because nobody wants to buy a bond paying 5 percent if other equally secure investments are paying 7 percent. So the face value of the bond goes down until its "effective yield," based on its market value rather than its face value, is equal to competing investments. Similarly, when interest rates go down, the value of a bond goes up. If interest rates drop to 3 percent, a bond paying 5 percent is more valuable, and investors will be willing to pay more than its face value to own it.

One need not be a bondholder to be affected by interest-rate fluctuations. In the early 1980s, a relative of one of the authors bought a house at a time when real estate prices were rising quickly and interest rates, partly in response to the demand for mortgages, were also heading up. She paid $140,000 for the house on the assumption that, once renovated, it would be worth $200,000. She took out a short-term loan with a variable interest rate. Her plan was to convert the loan into a larger one (in the form of a fixed-rate mortgage) once the renovation was complete and the home's value had risen as a result. The mortgage would more than cover the cost of the renovation. She would then live in part of the house and rent the rest of it, with the monthly income covering the mortgage payment.

Did this investor know what she owned? Yes and no. She knew that she owned a house that had a certain market value and that, barring a collapse in real estate prices, she could improve that market value by renovating it. But she didn't know, or didn't fully appreciate, that her house was more than a simple real estate investment. It was also a play on interest rates that, shortly after the purchase was made, began spinning upwards at a dizzying pace. During the six months it took for the renovation to be completed, interest rates doubled. When she went to convert her loan into a mortgage, she discovered the monthly payments would be twice what she expected—and considerably more than she could afford.

This investor knew when she opted to take a variable-rate mortgage that she was placing a bet on the direction of interest rates. Her bet was that rates would stay the same or, at worst, increase only slightly. As it happened, she lost the bet.

Her vulnerability was extreme. A professional investor never puts more than 15 percent of her portfolio into one asset. This amateur investor had put 100 percent of her wealth into a single bet on real estate and interest rates—and, exacerbating her risk even further, she was leveraged to the hilt. It was almost as risky as Anthony Richards's decision to risk his entire life savings on one roll of the dice in Las Vegas. If her relative had not bailed her out, she would have had to sell the property at a loss and been pushed into bankruptcy.

This story gets to the heart of what we mean by "know what you own." The reason this is the first rule of risk is that you can't assess the risk of your investment portfolio until you have a deep understanding of what factors affect it.

In the case of the house buyer, the important risk factor was the interest rate, which was rising at the time the investment was made. If she had done scenario analysis in advance, she could have determined the point at which the rate would become too high for her to manage. Knowing that, she could then have decided whether she believed it was likely or unlikely that rates might rise to that level. She might have decided that it was unlikely but still possible. Then she could have hedged her bet by taking all or part of the initial loan at a fixed rate. The extra cost of a fixed rate, versus the lower variable rate, would have been her insurance policy against a possible rise in interest rates.

Interest-rate exposure often leads to liquidity problems, one of the most dangerous threats to the solvency of investors, both small and large. In the case of our home buyer, her house did indeed rise in value, just as she had calculated; but that value on paper didn't help her make her monthly mortgage payments. On a much larger scale, Bunker and Herbert Hunt, sons of the Texan oil tycoon H.L. Hunt, acquired about a third of the world's silver supply during the 1970s, in the process driving up the price from $1.50 to $50 an ounce. When the price plunged 80 percent over a few days, they were obliged to cover a margin call of $3 billion on forward contracts. Although the Hunt brothers were worth more than $3 billion at the time, their wealth was not in easily liquidated assets. As a result, they went bankrupt.

Understanding our liquidity is a key aspect of knowing what we own. A bond or stock can be sold in a minute or two. A piece of real estate might take months to unload. Everyone has unexpected cash needs occasionally. All investors should know how long it will take to unwind a portfolio, or part of it, if such a need arises.

Rather than make the effort to understand the basic principles of investment and to analyze scenarios and consider potential upsides and downsides, many people choose to turn all their financial decision-making over to professional advisors, sometimes with disastrous results.

Ignorance is the most dangerous of all the risks that affect one's financial well-being, and it is a mystery why it remains so widespread. Doctors, whose authority in years past was rarely questioned, now find that many of their patients have scoured the Internet for information, are well informed about their symptoms, and have opinions on which drugs or other therapies might alleviate them. Yet the same people who are ready to take charge of their physical health are too often prepared to turn over responsibility for their financial health to an advisor without even verifying that person's qualifications.

There's something about financial matters that seems to turn off the brains of otherwise highly competent and intelligent individuals. They are too quick to defer to those who can toss around financial jargon and claim to have knowledge of future economic trends. They refuse to inform themselves about investment fundamentals despite the ready availability of information aimed specifically at non-experts in books, magazines, and daily newspapers.

Why is ignorance so dangerous? Because, while a doctor who does not have her patient's best interests at heart is a rarity, such is not the case when it comes to financial advisors. Some of them put their own interests ahead of their clients'.

Stephany Grasset, a retired Vancouver nursing instructor with special expertise in gerontology, is an example of a poorly informed investor. She is well educated, highly intelligent, and tough-minded. Yet, she admits, when the talk turns to stocks and bonds, "my eyes glaze over."

In 1998, she became dissatisfied with an advisor who had lost some of her money in an offshore investment. Her son, working in Ontario, recommended an advisor there who had done well for him during the stock market boom of the time. This person, although not licensed to practise in British Columbia, flew to Vancouver to pitch her services to a potentially lucrative client.

Grasset was impressed. "She was a very charming, very attractive, very bright woman," she explains. (Grasset did not wish to name the advisor because, at the time of writing, her case was under investigation.)

Grasset turned over more than $200,000. "This was money I earned by working hard for many years," she points out. "I didn't inherit anything." Over a period of six years, about $150,000 of those hard-earned savings disappeared.

For a person in her seventies, preserving capital is of prime importance. Typically, a person in Grasset's position would have a conservative portfolio consisting mainly of fixed-income investments, and perhaps a few blue-chip, dividend-paying stocks. Instead, this advisor placed the money in a bewildering array of mutual funds, many of them risky and volatile technology and country-specific funds. These investments were utterly inappropriate for a retiree. Worse, Grasset's account appears to have been "churned," meaning that money was moved in and out of different funds for no apparent reason other than to accumulate sales fees for the advisor.

Did Stephany Grasset know what she owned? Did she understand the risks she was exposed to? "I never even looked," she admits.

Her story, sadly enough, is not unusual. That was demonstrated in June 2005, when 500 angry investors crammed into the CBC building in Toronto for an Investors' Town Hall convened by David Brown, then the chairman of the Ontario Securities Commission. The meeting heard many horror stories, such as that of an elderly woman who lost U.S.$380,000 in an investment that had been sold to her as guaranteed. The worst story of all to emerge at the meeting was that the investment industry is weakly regulated and that the victims of dishonest players are rarely compensated for their losses.

Linda Leatherdale, who covered the meeting for the *Toronto Sun,* concluded: "You can go to jail for robbing a bank. But steal an investor's life savings, and you can go on to rip off more victims while you're under investigation. Then, it may be just a slap on the wrist, or lose your licence and maybe face a fine. But the victim never sees a dime of the money."

This is a huge risk factor for investors. Just as war, in the famous words of Georges Clemenceau, a French prime minister, is too important to be left to the generals, our financial affairs are too important to be left to the advisors. If the owner of the money doesn't have sufficient knowledge to ask the right questions of his advisor and to be able to distinguish an honest advisor from the other kind, his financial future is in peril.

Besides ignorance and unscrupulous investment advisors, another major risk facing Canadian investors today is the investment vehicle most of them rely upon, namely the mutual fund. When we put money in a mutual fund we are hiring a professional to take care of it and make it grow. This makes us feel confident about our savings—and that, ironically, is precisely why mutual funds are risky. Because investors have engaged a professional money manager, many are lulled into a false sense of security. Few take the trouble to understand how the fund industry actually works. As a result, they don't know what they own.

When you buy a stock, you own a piece of the company that issued it. When you buy units of a mutual fund, you own pieces of many different stocks and bonds into which the mutual fund manager has put his unitholders' money. But there is another crucial difference between a stock and a mutual fund. You pay a commission to the broker who sells you 500 shares of the Royal Bank, but that is the end of it. You then become one of the Royal Bank's owners and you pay nothing else unless you decide to sell your shares.

But if you own units of a mutual fund, you never stop paying. Whether the fund goes up or down, the company that manages it extracts money from your account every day, as long as you remain invested, in the form of a management fee or "management expense ratio" (MER). A share is a share, but a mutual fund is a "product"—the mutual fund itself, whose primary purpose, like that of any product, is to earn profits for those who produce it and those who sell it. Funds are designed for that purpose and they are highly efficient at it.

Mutual funds were invented in the nineteenth century but they did not achieve prominence until the 1980s, when North America's huge baby boom generation began saving for retirement. On the face of it, a mutual fund is easy for the average investor to understand, which may partly explain why millions of people have pumped billions of dollars into funds over the past two decades.

A mutual fund pools many small amounts of money, contributed by individuals, into a large amount. It hires a professional investment manager who uses that large pool of money to buy a diversified portfolio of investments on behalf of the unitholders. A mutual fund thereby gives the average person access to professional money management, something previously reserved for the very rich, as well as a degree of investment diversification that such a person could not achieve on his or her own.

That's the story that has been sold with stunning effectiveness by the mutual fund industry, and it's true. But it's not the whole story. If you own units of mutual funds and that's all you know about them, then you don't know what you own.

The definition (by the industry itself) of funds as products means they cannot always be managed in a rational way. Suppose you are the manager of a "product" that has been sold to the public as an Asian mutual fund—that is, one that invests solely in companies based in Asia. It is your responsibility to deliver the product you have sold. The fund there-fore must be invested in Asian stocks, even if there are no Asian stocks that the manager wants to buy at current prices.

Perhaps there are only a dozen Asian stocks that the manager likes, but he has too much money to confine himself to just a few. In addition, the mutual fund has promised its customers diversification, and it must deliver on that promise. So the manager buys some other stocks that he doesn't like as much—and maybe even some that he doesn't like at all.

In other words, what is advertised as the prime virtue of mutual funds—that they pool small amounts of money into a large amount—is also a major flaw. It all but guarantees that you, the unitholder, will own bad stocks. Few investors are aware of this. If they were, they might be less eager to invest in mutual funds.

A mutual fund is indeed a product, but not in the way our favourite breakfast cereal is. The cereal always tastes the same. The fund, because it is a financial instrument, is in constant flux. An invest-ment style that worked one year won't work as well the next, and so it may be changed. The manager who achieved above-average returns may have left; as a result, the fund is not the same this year as it was last year. If you think it is, you don't know what you own.

The biggest risk associated with mutual funds is not that the manager who picks the stocks won't do a good job of investing, but that the advisor who sells it is compensated, not by you the investor, but by the mutual fund company. This creates an obvious conflict of interest: rather than put the client in the best fund for that client, the advisor may be tempted to sell the fund that creates the most income for himself. An important aspect of knowing what you own is knowing who gets paid for what.

If Stephany Grasset's advisor had had her client's best interests at heart, she might have placed her money with a company such as Vancouver-based Phillips, Hager & North (PH&N), one of a handful of no-load, low-fee mutual fund operators in Canada. The PH&N Dividend Income Fund, one of the steadiest performers among the 5,000 or so Canadian mutual funds, would be a good place for some of a retiree's assets. It is invested in conservative, dividend-paying companies and yet has a better rate of return than many funds invested in speculative securities. From the advisor's standpoint, however, there is a big problem with PH&N—it won't pay a cent to a financial advisor.

A telltale set of initials recurs throughout Grasset's investment statements, attached to the names of the various mutual funds in which her money was placed:

DSC, which stands for *deferred sales charge,* meaning that Grasset had to pay the fund company a percentage of the assets originally invested if she sold her units in a fund. (A no-load fund company, such as PH&N, Mawer Investment Management, or Saxon Mutual Funds, charges no such commissions.)

The DSC, invented by Mackenzie Financial in 1987, was one of the best things that ever happened to the mutual fund industry and one of the worst that ever happened to investors. Previously, mutual fund investors had to pay a sales commission consisting of 9 percent of their investment at the time of purchase. Because the commission, also known as a "front-end load," was so high, mutual funds were a hard sell. Jim O'Donnell, who ran Mackenzie, realized it would be much easier to sell funds if there were no visible sales charge.

So instead of giving the financial advisors a 9 percent commission paid directly by the customer, Mackenzie paid them 5 percent, which it took out of the money extracted as management fees from customers' assets. In addition, the advisors collected a "trailer fee" consisting of one-half of one percent of the customer's assets annually for as long as the customer stayed invested in the fund. This money also comes out of the management fee. The DSC kicks in only if the fund is sold in less than seven years.

The DSC was indeed a smart move—Mackenzie doubled its sales in the year after it was adopted—and much of the industry soon followed its example. The reason the DSC is bad news for investors is the same reason that it boosted sales—it makes the sales commission invisible. All that the typical customer knows is that she doesn't have to pay any sales commission unless she sells the fund. She doesn't know that her advisor got 5 percent as soon as she turned over her money and that she will pay for this through management fees that will reduce the returns she gets from her investment. She doesn't know that an unscrupulous advisor has an incentive to cash in the $10,000 the investor had put in Fund A and transfer the money to Fund B for no other reason than to pocket another invisible $500 sales commission.

Most advisors do not behave in this way. But the compensation system provides an incentive for those who are so inclined. Investors who do not make the effort to understand how the mutual fund industry works are lambs to be fleeced by this kind of advisor.

Steve Wynn, a Las Vegas casino developer, once said, "If you want to make money in a casino, own one." The same advice applies to mutual funds. Just like a casino owner, the owner of a mutual fund company makes money—from management fees— whether or not his customers do. For Canadian mutual funds, management fees are typically around 2.5 percent of the assets invested per year. This sounds like a small number but in fact it is a large one—as can be seen when it is expressed, not as a percentage of the assets but, more to the point, as a percentage of the *return* on those assets.

Suppose the stock market had a flat year and on December 31 its overall value was the same as it had been on January 1. Suppose also that your fund manager was able, through shrewd investing, to beat the market by 2.5 percent. The statement you receive from the fund company would show a return of zero percent for the year. But, in fact, your investment was up by 2.5 percent; the management fee (invisible on mutual fund company statements) ate up 100 percent of your gain. The investor who gets into the habit of calculating management fees in this way understands how significant, and damaging to his financial well-being, they really are.

No-load funds such as PH&N are sold directly to the public. Because they do not have to pay commissions or trailer fees to salespersons, they are able to charge lower management fees. This does not guarantee that they will outperform the high-fee funds, but it gives them an edge. And as an investor in a difficult and unpredictable financial world, you need every edge you can get.

Mutual fund companies and the financial advisors who sell their products try to minimize the impact of fees when their customers raise the subject, but the facts are undeniable. Every dollar extracted from your retirement account is a dollar that does not get a chance to compound and multiply over the life of your RRSP. That is why the impact of fees over the long term is so dramatic.

Suppose you invested $100,000 in a balanced fund (one that contains both stocks and bonds) and kept it there for twenty years. The average Canadian balanced fund comes with an MER of 2.43 percent. The PH&N balanced fund has a comparatively puny MER of 0.89 percent. Let's also assume that both the average balanced fund and the PH&N fund had identical pre–MER returns of 7 percent a year. At the end of twenty years, your $100,000 would have swollen to $244,423 in the average fund. In the PH&N fund it would have grown to $327,436.

That's a difference of $83,000. The essential point here is that neither fund had superior investment management. They both returned 7 percent a year before fees. The only difference was one and a half percentage points in the management fee. Of course the fund companies know this, and most of them would like to reduce their MERs. But they can't because, except for the handful that sell their funds direct to the consumer, fund companies depend on independent salespersons. And the salespersons won't move product unless they are well paid for doing so. Those payments come out of the MER.

It is crucial, if we are truly to know what we own, that we understand that a mutual fund is not just a basket of stocks and bonds. It is, as the fund industry frankly concedes, a "product" designed to make money for the "manufacturer" (the fund company) and the "retailer" (the investment advisor who sells it). The risk posed to investors by mutual fund fees is especially acute in Canada where these fees, on average, are almost twice as high as those in the U.S.

A particularly egregious example of advisor greed came to light in 2005. Some funds are sold in two versions—one with no sales commission but a higher management fee, and one with a DSC (deferred sales charge) but a lower management fee. Without telling their clients, some advisors switched their money into the higher-fee version once the DSC had fallen to zero (because it had been invested for six years). This was the most blatant example imaginable of the inherent conflict of interest between mutual fund salespersons and clients—the client gets a lower return because he pays a higher MER, but the advisor gets more money because the high–MER version of the same fund pays him a higher trailer fee.

Another way in which mutual fund fees add to investor risk is the pressure they put on the stock pickers who manage the high-fee funds. In order to compensate for the burden of the MER, the manager may be tempted to make risky investments in order to boost his fund's performance. Yet even when he has a big win—a stock that triples or quadruples in value—it may not have much impact on a huge fund that owns 200 stocks because the mediocre performers drag down the fund's overall performance.

Yet another risk factor for mutual fund investors is the phenomenon of "closet indexing." This term refers to a situation in which an actively managed fund mirrors its benchmark stock index. Many large Canadian equity funds fall into this category. One way to find out if the fund you own is in this category is to consult the Globefund.com Web site. Look up your fund and then generate a ten-year chart comparing it with the appropriate benchmark index. For example, if it's a Canadian equity fund, compare it to the TSX composite index. If the two lines on the chart coincide, chances are you own a closet index fund.

Managers of these funds deliberately emulate the index rather than take big bets on certain stocks in an attempt to do better than the index. This is an act of self-preservation. Customers tend to withdraw their money if their fund underperforms the index, and the surest way not to underperform the index is to duplicate it.

Why is this risky for investors? Because it is always risky not to know what we own. As we will see in Chapter 5, index funds can be a useful alternative to managed mutual funds. But if we are going to own one, it should be a deliberate choice. As we have just seen, fees eat away at our investments. The median MER for Canadian equity funds was 2.64 percent as of April 2005. In contrast, the i60, an exchange-traded index fund (ETF) that owns the 60 largest stocks on the Toronto Stock Exchange in proportion to their market capitalization, carries a tiny MER of only 0.17 percent. If you are going to buy an index fund, it makes no sense to buy one with a high fee when you can get the same thing for a fraction of the price.

If your investments are in mutual funds, the first important step is to understand how the mutual fund industry works. Ideally, you will then be well enough informed to manage your investments for yourself, eliminating the expensive middleman and taking advantage of low-cost alternatives to high-fee mutual funds.

The next step is to understand what risks your money is exposed to in the investments it has been placed in. To see how you might approach this task,

ACTIVE RISK

There's a kind of risk most investors have never heard of. Steve Rice, vice-president of Canadian index services at Standard & Poor's, the New York-based provider of credit ratings and equity research, calls it "active risk." He means the risk that a mutual fund run by a stock-picking manager won't beat its benchmark stock market index. This is serious because it costs an investor more to own an actively-managed fund than one that passively mirrors the index. Some actively managed funds do beat the index from time to time but they are hard to find. Over the past three years, only 6% of diversified Canadian equity funds managed to do it.

let's take a look at the investment portfolio of a typical Canadian family whose case was described in 2004 in a personal-finance column in *The Toronto Star*. The couple, identified as Phil and Iris, are in their late forties and have three children. Phil has $73,000 in an RRSP invested in six mutual funds from

Investors Group, a Winnipeg-based company that maintains its own dedicated sales force to sell its own funds. Iris has $71,000 in her RRSP, invested in the same Investors Group funds.

In gaining a deep knowledge of what we own in our investments, one of the key factors to analyze is the extent of our diversification. As children we learned a fundamental life rule: *Don't Put All Your Eggs in One Basket.* In the world of investment, not putting all your eggs in one basket means diversifying among different kinds of investments, different industrial sectors, and different geographical regions. Investing without diversifying is like going out on the ocean in a rowboat without a life preserver.

Diversification gives us stability and a kind of insurance. If energy stocks go down, maybe financial ones will go up. If most stocks go down, perhaps bonds will go up. Even if they don't, we know that a $10,000 bond will be worth $10,000 when it matures. If the U.S. stock market tanks, maybe markets elsewhere in the world will do well.

The benefits of diversification seem self-evident, yet many investors lack the self-discipline to take advantage of them. They are attracted to the hottest sector and can't resist the temptation to maximize their returns by putting all their money into it. In the technology boom of the late 1990s, it took considerable self-discipline to keep any money in the stocks of well-established, profitable companies when those stocks had single-digit growth rates and paid single-digit dividends at a time when the Altamira e-business fund boasted a one-year return of 188 percent. Both authors are acquainted with individuals who suffered massive, permanent loss of capital when the technology sector crashed. These were intelligent individuals who would not have dreamt of gambling their life savings in a casino or failing to purchase fire insurance for their homes. Yet they were wholly invested in technology without realizing that such behaviour had more in common with that of a roulette player than a rational investor.

Phil and Iris are not so foolish. Their six Investors funds give them exposure to Canadian, American, and European stocks. Two of their funds contain fixed-income investments, another specializes in dividend-paying stocks, and another is in science and technology. So they own six different baskets. All the baskets, because they are mutual funds with dozens of different holdings, are filled with many eggs. In that sense, Phil and Iris are well diversified.

In another important sense, however, they are not diversified enough. Both have the same investment advisor who works for Investors Group. Not surprisingly, all their funds are offerings of that company. This is bad. Different mutual fund companies have different investment styles. Sometimes, one company will be in a slump while another will enjoy a hot streak. If you are going to put your money in high-fee mutual funds (which we do not recommend), you need to diversify among fund companies.

As it happens, Phil and Iris's funds are a pretty mediocre bunch, in large part because their higher-than-average fees act as a brake on performance. The European Equity Fund, for example, has an excessive MER of 3.09 percent and tends to underperform the European index by about that amount. Phil and Iris would be better off in a European index fund. They are in the Investors fund instead because that is the brand their advisor sells.

Besides the high MER, there are other risks that come with this fund. For example, you're exposed to foreign-exchange risk; if European currencies weaken, so does the value of your investment. And the top holdings in the Investors European fund include major European oil companies. Because oil companies operate in U.S. dollars, you also have exposure to that currency. This means that the success of your investment will depend on how well the Canadian dollar fares against other currencies. It may be that the fund manager has taken steps to protect his investors against this sort of risk. If so, your financial advisor can explain this to you. If he can't, you may wish to consider finding an advisor who can.

None of these risks are reasons not to buy the fund, but you need to be aware of them and decide how much exposure to them you are comfortable with. If your advisor is proposing an investment, ask him such questions as, "What risks is this investment exposed to?" and "How will this investment change the overall risk profile of my portfolio?" Challenge the advisor's answers. Try to answer the questions yourself. If you aren't satisfied that you know as much as you need to, you shouldn't make the investment. Too often we are sold financial products whose risks are not fully understood, whether by us or the salesperson. If you think that a European equity fund is simply a basket of stocks in European companies, then you don't know what you own.

On closer examination, it emerges that this couple's funds are not giving them as much diversification as they think. Some 80 percent of their holdings are in three Canadian funds, all of which have large positions in the major Canadian banks. If you are going to be heavily exposed to one sector, the highly profitable Canadian banking oligopoly is a good one to be exposed to. But even Canadian banks sometimes go through rough patches, and diversification is all about not being overly dependent on the success of any one sector.

A good example of the risk of accidental non-diversification occurred in the summer of 2005, when the rapid rise of oil prices in turn lifted energy stocks to new highs. A mutual fund investor who held an energy fund could rightly assume that he had that sector well covered. But what if he also had a general Canadian equity fund, as well as a balanced fund and perhaps an income trust fund? All of these would also contain oil and gas stocks, given the prominent role these stocks play in Canadian equity markets.

Without knowing it, this investor would be dangerously overexposed to the volatile energy sector because of the chameleon-like nature of mutual funds. Having several different baskets doesn't give us diversification if the baskets contain too many identical eggs. It gives us the opposite, overspecialization, which increases the volatility and therefore the riskiness of our portfolio. For real diversification we need different baskets *and* different eggs.

The hedge fund is a more complex version of the mutual fund. A hedge fund is so called because it is supposed to be a way of "hedging," or offsetting, the risk of holding a portfolio of conventional stocks and bonds. Your hedge fund, in theory, goes up when your other investments go down.

A hedge fund is typically more aggressive than a mutual fund in seeking positive returns for its investors. The mutual fund manager is judged by his performance relative to his benchmark index. For example, a fund invested in stocks of large American companies would be compared to the Dow Jones Industrial Average. If the Dow was down 10 percent on the year and the fund was down only 5 percent, the fund manager would be considered to have done well. Not so for a hedge fund—its goal is to produce profits regardless of whether the stock market is up or down.

In order to achieve that goal, a hedge fund manager has more tools at his disposal than a mutual fund manager, who is restricted to buying and selling stocks. The hedge fund manager can go "short"—that is, make a bet that a stock will go down in value. He does this by selling the stock first and buying it later at, he hopes, a lower price than he sold it for. (Some Canadian mutual funds have recently received regulatory approval to sell short on a limited basis.)

As well as stocks, the hedge fund manager can trade all kinds of financial instruments, including commodities, currencies, and derivatives. In addition, the hedge fund can borrow money to buy investments, thereby unleashing the power of leverage to get bigger returns.

Hedge funds are more complex than mutual funds, but are they always more risky? Not necessarily. In fact, it is quite possible for a hedge fund to be less risky than a bond fund, one of the most conservative of investments. Hedge funds are neither inherently more nor less risky than other investments. For the investor, the challenge is to identify the dangerous ones before committing money to them.

One writer, Colin Anthony, holds the view that hedge funds are actually less risky than ordinary mutual funds, whose very simplicity increases the risks associated with them. Using an automotive analogy similar to the one that opened this chapter, he likens a conventional equity fund—which can bet only that stocks will rise even when the market as a whole is moving downward—to driving a car without any brakes.

The hedge fund manager, on the other hand, does have brakes at his disposal. He can avoid a crash by dumping all his shares, whereas a mutual fund manager, because he is running an equity fund "product," is expected to remain invested. Moreover, because he is unrestricted in his ability to sell short, the hedge fund manager, unlike his mutual fund counterpart, can make big profits when the market is heading south. On the other hand, a hedge fund that uses leverage, thereby enhancing potential losses as well as potential gains, might increase the overall risk of your portfolio.

Originally hedge funds were intended for wealthy investors who, presumably, know what they are doing. However, the amazing case of Long Term Capital Management (LTCM), a disaster created in 1994 by some of the best financial minds in the U.S., proved that wealthy investors can be just as clueless as small investors.

John Meriwether, an experienced bond trader from Salomon Brothers, was in charge of LTCM. Also involved were two economists, Myron Scholes and Robert Merton, who had won Nobel prizes for their work on risk. Another partner in the venture was David Mullins, former vice-chairman of the Federal Reserve Board, the U.S. central bank.

Little wonder, with such respected financial brains at the helm, that Long Term Capital Management was able to recruit eighty investors to put up a minimum of $10 million each. Merrill Lynch, a major investment dealer, and the Union Bank of Switzerland bought shares to sell to their own clients. LTCM's initial capitalization was $1.3 billion.

The plan was to make "convergence trades." This

meant finding securities, usually government bonds, that were underpriced or overpriced by very small amounts relative to one another. The fund managers would then buy the cheap ones and sell the over-priced ones short. The market would eventually price the securities accurately and LTCM would benefit. According to Scholes, LTCM would be like a vacuum cleaner sucking up the nickels others couldn't see.

LTCM had to take large bets with borrowed money in order to make the kinds of profits its investors expected. At first, the plan worked brilliantly. During its first two years, shareholders enjoyed returns in excess of 40 percent. LTCM was so successful that, in 1998, it decided it had too much money and returned some of it to its investors.

Later that year, LTCM could have used that capital, because it experienced a major liquidity crisis. Russia defaulted on its debt, an event that unsettled international financial markets in ways that LTCM had not anticipated. Because of a flight to U.S. dollars, all non-dollar-denominated securities were suddenly moving in the same direction—down. And all of LTCM's bets on correlations between various international securities went out the window. Because the fund was so highly leveraged, every one-dollar drop in one of its holdings meant a loss of $100. LTCM suffered a swift meltdown.

As Paul Krugman, the Princeton University economist and *New York Times* columnist, points out, "Everyone knows that there are potential events that are not likely to happen but will have very big effects on financial markets if they do. A realistic assessment of risk should take into account the possibility of these large, low-probability events."

Because LTCM's managers failed to do this, writes Krugman, "they greatly understated the risk to which they were exposing both their investors and those who lent them money."

It would be wrong to accuse LTCM of incompetence. It had a good business plan and the financial wizards running it had thought carefully about risk. But they hadn't considered one major risk: that if all the markets they were operating in moved in one direction simultaneously, they could lose big time.

This lesson applies to all investors. Few of us are likely to invest millions in exotic financial instruments such as LTCM. But it is the unexpected risk—such as being unwittingly overexposed to energy because we don't understand the composition of our mutual funds—that can be devastating.

In times of crisis in the international financial markets, there is a flight to U.S. dollars. LTCM ignored the possibility of this scenario occurring. Had it taken it into account, it might have followed the same strategy but with a reduced position, so that even in a liquidity crunch the fund would not have gone broke. As we shall see in the next chapter, the ability to visualize multiple future scenarios is an essential part of effective investing.

To avoid a collapse of the LTCM fund, which might have triggered an international financial crisis, the Federal Reserve Bank of New York organized a rescue operation in which several banks put $3.5 billion into the fund and took over its management. LTCM was liquidated in 2000.

The LTCM debacle is stunning proof of the importance of our first rule. Huge institutions and wealthy investors put vast sums into this mysterious operation without knowing what they owned. In fact, they weren't even allowed to find out. "The fund's operations were carried out in absolute secrecy," reported *Le Monde Diplomatique* in November 1998. "Investors who asked questions were told to take their money somewhere else." These supposedly sophisticated investors, points out Krugman, "failed to ask even the simplest questions such as, 'How much money have you borrowed from other people?'"

Whenever hedge funds get into serious trouble, the two culprits that laid LTCM low are usually responsible: too much leverage and too little liquidity. If wealthy, experienced investors can blunder into an investment they don't understand and lose their money, how dangerous must such investments be for small investors? Originally, hedge funds required large minimum investments intended to keep them off limits to people without the knowledge to protect themselves. Now, however, some hedge funds are being sold to people with as little as $500 to pony up. And some are being advertised, falsely, as risk free.

An example was Portus Alternative Management, a Toronto-based hedge fund whose structure was so complex that almost no one, including the dealers selling it, understood how it worked. Portus sold "principal-protected notes"—meaning that, if the notes were held for a minimum of five years, investors were assured of getting their money back. Meanwhile, the geniuses running the fund would use a portion of the invested money to make big returns. Maybe they would succeed, maybe they wouldn't—but at the very least, the investor's principal, so the story went, was as safe as if it were deposited in the bank.

Advisors who referred clients into Portus got a 4 percent commission for their efforts plus a one-percent trailer fee. These advisors had been assured by Portus that their clients' principal was fully protected. But this was not the case—there was no guarantee that the money was safe. Securities regulators investigated Portus and, in February 2005, abruptly closed it down, leaving some 30,000 investors wondering if they would ever again see the total of about $800 million they had invested in the fund. As of the summer of 2005, investigators were trying to figure out where the investors' money was, and why much of it had wound up outside the country.

Thelma van der Steen, a seventy-four-year-old Toronto woman, invested $60,000, a large part of her savings, in Portus under the impression that it was as safe as a guaranteed income certificate. "To me, hedges are something that's in the garden," she told *The Globe and Mail.* "I'm not too familiar with them. But he [her financial advisor] showed us all these graphs and everything. I knew nothing about it."

The securities regulators investigating Portus were critical of the role of advisors in the fiasco. "If the shepherds had not herded the sheep to the slaughterhouse, they would still be alive," said Michael Watson, head of enforcement for the Ontario Securities Commission.

Like mutual funds, hedge funds charge fat fees— 2 percent of the investor's assets per year. In addition, unlike ordinary mutual funds, the manager gets a performance fee, usually 20 percent of the increase in value of the fund. This inflates the risk to investors because, while managers take home a share of the gains, their pay is not docked if there are losses. The Investment Dealers Association of Canada, which regulates brokerages, concluded in a report that this "asymmetry"—a reward for a win but no penalty for a loss—provides the hedge fund manager with "an incentive to take undue risks, including extensive use of leverage." Prospective investors should note that the same asymmetry applies to most hedge funds.

Not only that, said the report, but the principal-protected notes that are supposed to protect risk-averse investors are themselves risky. In most cases, these notes do not mature for about ten years, during which time most of the money has to be in some secure deposit to ensure the principal is protected. Only a small portion is invested aggressively, and this money is so encumbered with fees that investors may get little or no return. Tying up money for a decade and only getting the same money back, diminished in value by inflation, is "no small risk," the report correctly concluded.

Most hedge funds are easier to understand than LTCM or Portus. And many of them are perfectly legitimate investments. But there is no investment class where the "know what you own" principle is more important. The Ontario Teachers Pension Plan, with $84.3 billion under management, is one of the largest pension funds in Canada. It has about $4 billion in 100 different hedge funds, but not a penny is invested before a fund has been thoroughly investigated. The pension plan has seven staff members devoted to monitoring its hedge fund investments. "If you don't understand something, you don't do it," Bob Bertram, executive vice-president of Teachers, told *The Globe and Mail.*

All investors, large and small, should subscribe to that policy. As individual investors, we don't have experts to do the due diligence for us. But that shouldn't stop us from asking some tough questions. What kind of hedge fund is it? Does it reduce the risk of the rest of my portfolio by moving in a different direction? Or is it just a very aggressive mutual fund making risky bets on commodities and stocks? Why is my advisor recommending this particular fund as opposed to another? How much is my advisor being paid for selling this fund? What do I know about the company sponsoring the fund? What is the track record of the manager?

Ideally, the hedge fund investor would have easy access to information that tells her how the fund will react to various movements of major economic indicators. She could then compare that to similar information about her mutual funds, stocks, and fixed-income investments, thereby obtaining a clear understanding of her overall risk situation and the ability to adjust that risk as necessary in accordance with her own risk tolerance. Unfortunately, as we have already said, that information is not yet readily available.

Until it is, the best advice is to assess a hedge fund as you would assess an individual stock. Review its management and its past performance. Understand its style. Most importantly, understand what risk factors will affect its performance. Do the fund's managers and salespersons have this information? Are they willing to share it with you? If they are and you are considering investing, before you plunk down your money you might track the fund for a while and see how it does when the risk factors change. If you can't get the information you need, then you won't know what you own and you shouldn't invest.

Most investors had not heard of hedge funds until recently, and the same is true of that other hot investment vehicle of the times, the income trust. As is the case with hedge funds, many investors own income trusts without knowing what they actually are. Their confusion is understandable because income trusts behave like an amalgam of a stock and a bond. They represent ownership of a security and are traded on the stock exchange. On the other hand, they are, as their name suggests, primarily income-producing vehicles with yields well in excess of those currently available from bonds or bank term deposits.

Owning a unit of an income trust is like owning a share of an ordinary company. The difference is that, in the case of a trust, a portion of the cash flow from the underlying business flows directly to the unitholders, whereas an ordinary company retains that money and may or may not pay some of it as dividends to the shareholders. Because low interest rates have reduced returns available from bonds and other fixed-income investments, the popularity of income trusts has soared in recent years. Trusts typically offer yields of around 8 percent or higher, more than twice what is available from a long-term government bond. However, unlike a bond, a unit of an income trust carries no guarantee that it will retain its value. Just like ordinary shares, units in a trust can increase or decrease in value.

Income trusts were devised as a way of avoiding the double taxation imposed on business profits in Canada. Businesses have to pay corporate tax on their profits. When after-tax earnings are paid to shareholders as dividends, they are taxed again. In contrast, the distributions a trust pays to its unitholders are taxed only once, in the hands of the unitholder.

To illustrate the difference it helps to compare

the after-tax proceeds from $100 of business income paid to an investor by a trust to the same amount paid by a corporation. If the trust units were held in a non-taxable registered retirement savings plan (RRSP), the investor would get the full $100. A corporate dividend representing the same amount of business income would add only $58 to the investor's retirement account.

The first income trusts were in the resource and real estate industries. More recently, income trusts have been launched by businesses in such varied industries as restaurants, phone book publishing, coffee decaffeination, liquor retailing, and casinos. What these businesses have in common is large, stable, or growing cash flows sufficient to provide the regular distributions that income-trust investors want.

As with hedge funds, there are good trusts and bad ones. Trusts are a steady source of cash, which is a good reason for having some of them in your portfolio. But the appeal of income trusts—the generous income they provide—is also a risk factor. The president of one of Canada's largest real estate companies advised one of the authors that, when considering an investment in a real estate investment trust (REIT), one should always remember that a high yield is a danger sign. His company, he pointed out, invests millions annually to maintain its properties, often in the form of invisible upgrades to such things as elevators or plumbing systems. A REIT that is competing for investors by offering high yields might be tempted to skimp on such necessary expenditures in order to have more money to pass on to its unitholders. That kind of REIT will not have strong tenant loyalty and will be less able to weather an economic downturn than a more conservative one that maintains its buildings, even though that means it must offer lower yields. The buyer of the high-yield REIT may pay for the extra cash he receives now in the form of a capital loss (lower unit price) later.

A similar risk factor exists with respect to oil and gas trusts. When a well dries up, its operators are responsible for the big job of dismantling the facilities and cleaning up the site and the surroundings. Oil trusts are expected to put money aside for this job. But if they are paying too much in distributions, they may not be saving enough to meet their future obligations. In a time of rising energy prices and soaring profits for the oil and gas industry, it's tempting for executives to assume they will have no trouble paying the cleanup costs when obliged to. But in less buoyant times, millions of dollars of unfunded obligations could make the market nervous. If that happens, investors in oil and gas income trusts may see the value of their units decline.

Energy trusts usually have the highest yields because they are the most volatile, their profits being dependent on such unpredictable factors as the weather and Middle East politics. Also, these trusts can stay in business only as long as they have a supply of oil or gas; they have to find or buy new wells as existing ones run dry. This is a much iffier proposition than a trust based on a product in stable supply such as pizza or office buildings. That is why the yields are higher on energy trusts—investors are assuming more risk when they buy a conventional oil or gas trust. In contrast, Canadian Oil Sands Trust, which has massive reserves, also has a very low yield. This tells us that the market considers it a low-risk investment.

A fundamental risk that investors must address is that the income trust may not be operating a profitable business. It may be using the cash from new investors and lenders to pay high distributions to its existing unitholders. These high distributions in turn attract more investors, whose capital is then paid out in distributions. If an income trust is paying out more in distributions than its cash flow would normally allow, it is a pyramid scheme—and, like all pyramid schemes, it will eventually collapse.

To know what you are buying, therefore, the first question to ask is, "Are the managers of this income trust paying out more money than their business is earning?" Investment advisors and brokerage company analysts are paid to answer questions like this.

Second, you need to understand the underlying business. You are buying a trust primarily for income, with any capital gains being a bonus. This is the opposite of a stock, which is normally bought primarily for capital gains, with dividends as a bonus. So the big question is, can this company sustain the cash flow necessary to pay its distributions, not only in boom times but during economic doldrums also? How safe are these payments? What eventualities could cause a trust to reduce or even cancel its payments?

To answer such questions, you will have to do the kind of scenario planning we will discuss in the next chapter. Just as an example, let's consider the case of Priszm Canadian Income Fund, one of the largest KFC (Kentucky Fried Chicken) franchisees in the world with 481 restaurants across Canada.

Like all investments, Priszm has an upside and a downside. The upside is that its KFC brand is a household name, it has a massive presence in the fast food market covering all parts of the country, and it has sound management that does not rest on its laurels. It regularly upgrades its premises and adds new menu items such as the barbequed ribs that in 2005 became its first non-chicken offering.

The downside is that Canada, like all the industrialized countries, has an aging population, and older people tend to prefer lighter foods than fried chicken—which, despite an expanded menu, is still KFC's trademark item.

A more dangerous potential downside is the threat of bird flu. What if this deadly disease swept through North America, requiring affected chicken populations to be eradicated? Priszm's restaurants might then be hit by a chicken shortage. Or perhaps consumers would not wish to eat chicken at all. These are remote possibilities, but thinking about remote possibilities is an essential part of effective scenario planning.

Even assuming no such disastrous events, Priszm might be viewed as a riskier investment than other choices available to investors interested in the food-service industry. That is because Prizsm is a franchisee, meaning that it owns the KFC restaurants and pays distributions out of its profits. Expenses such as marketing and capital improvements could reduce those profits, thereby also reducing distributions.

In contrast, several competitors have been set up as "royalty income trusts." Typically, all that these trusts own are the trademarks of the restaurants, which they lease back to the franchisor. The franchisees who own and operate the restaurants pay a royalty based on a percentage of their sales, a portion of which flows to the unitholders in the trust. So, assuming sales are at least maintained, the unitholders collect the same amount, even if expenses cut into the restaurants' profits. That is because the distributions are paid out of sales, not profits. In financial jargon, these are "top-line" trusts, whereas Priszm is a "bottom-line" trust.

Finally, a fundamental risk that income trust investors must consider is the outlook for interest rates. A sharp rise would make such investments as bank guaranteed investment certificates and money market funds more competitive with income trusts. These investments, unlike income trusts, are risk free, and if the spread between income trust yields and no-risk yields narrows, many investors will dump their trust units, sending valuations down.

One reason that it is difficult to know what you own is that even something as basic as a mortgage has become increasingly complex in recent years. This is a good thing because different borrowers have different needs, and modern financial technology allows lenders to customize their products in ways that were not previously possible. In fact, as such technology advances, every mortgage may be customized for the individual.

In the meantime, a typical lender, Canadian Imperial Bank of Commerce (CIBC), offers its customers eight different mortgages. Remember, the whole point of gaining a deep understanding of what we own is so that we can realistically assess the risks to which we are exposed. If we want to understand these risks, we must pay as much attention to the debit side of our personal balance sheet as to the asset side. Just as owning an oil stock exposes us to oil-price risk, so being a borrower exposes us to interest rate risk.

When you take out a mortgage, you have to consider various scenarios regarding the direction of interest rates. For example, if you think current rates are too low to last, the bank offers a fixed-rate closed mortgage with a term of one, two, three, four, five, seven, or ten years. If, on the other hand, you think rates may fall but you want the option of changing your mind, you can choose a "convertible" mortgage that is closed for six months after which it can be locked in at then-prevailing rates. Finally, a borrower confident that rates will stay low would opt for a fully open mortgage.

CIBC even offers a mortgage in which the borrower earns frequent-flier points for his interest payments. However, this "AeroMortgage" carries a higher interest rate than other of the bank's offerings such as the "Better Than Prime Mortgage." Imagine the calculations a borrower would have to make before deciding whether to take this mortgage or the one with the lower rate. What will those airline points be worth in the future? Will air fares go up, or will they fall? What will happen to the oil price, the prime determinant of air fares? Will the airline honouring the frequent-flier points still be in business when I want to travel? How much money would I save at the lower interest rate, and how many airline tickets could I buy with that money?

These questions all involve predictions about the future. In fact, every financial move we make, whether investing in an income trust or taking out a mortgage, is a bet on the future. The key to being a good investor is understanding the bet you are taking. That means knowing what your investment portfolio actually contains, and knowing what risk factors could affect it and by how much. When you know that, you will understand what you own. Then you will be ready to formulate the scenarios that will help you manage your risk as the future unfolds.

THE BOTTOM LINE

Financial instruments are in a state of constant flux, so what we own in our investment portfolios changes from day to day.

The more complex the financial instrument, the more difficult it is to know what you own. We don't need to know exactly what is in a mutual fund but we do need to know how various risk factors will affect it. Knowing what you own means knowing your risk. And it means knowing your liquidity—how long will it take you to turn your investment into cash if that becomes necessary?

Ignorance is the most dangerous risk. Our financial well-being is too important to entrust it entirely to an advisor. Anyone who can read can become well-informed about the fundamentals of investing.

If you own shares, you are the owner of a small piece of a company. If you own mutual fund units, you own a "product" designed to make money for fund companies and financial advisors. To know how much owning a mutual fund really costs, investors should calculate fund fees as a percentage of the annual return, not as a percentage of the amount invested in the fund.

Some mutual funds mirror their benchmark indices. There is no point in paying a high price for active management if you are not getting it. Investors in such funds would be better off buying a real index fund at a much lower cost.

A hedge fund is so-called because it is supposed to go up when other investments such as mutual funds go down. Hedge funds are more complex than mutual funds but they are not necessarily more risky. A big advantage is that they can take major "short" positions, allowing them to make money when the stock market is in decline. Some hedge funds are good and some are disasters. Investors need to do thorough research before investing in them.

Income trusts are a steady source of cash, which is a good reason for including them in your portfolio. But, although income trusts are usually bought for yield, they are not the same as other cash-generating investments such as bonds or money market funds. Income trust units are like shares—they can go down in value.

Every financial move we make is a bet on the future. As with any bet, we might win or we might lose. They key to being a good investor is understanding your bets and that means knowing what is actually in your portfolio and what risk factors could affect it.

three

USE MULTIPLE SCENARIOS, NOT FORECASTS

QLT INC. is a Vancouver drug developer whose best-known product is Visudyne, a treatment for wet age-related macular degeneration, a vision-damaging eye disease that afflicts many old people.

As the senior population increases, so does the incidence of macular degeneration and the market for a drug like Visudyne. Obviously, QLT is on to a good thing. In the vast majority of countries around the world, both the average age and the percentage of persons over sixty-five are increasing. Europe and Japan are the oldest societies, followed by the U.S., Canada, and Australia. Less-developed countries like Jamaica and Bangladesh are still comparatively young, but they too will have aging populations later in the century. In such a demographic environment, the future for a drug like Visudyne seems bright indeed.

As of 2004, Visudyne had been approved in seventy countries, including Japan with its huge market of seniors. In that year, the U.S. government approved it for reimbursement under its Medicare and Medicaid programs. These were among the reasons, in a 2004 report, analyst Karen Boodram of Pacific International Securities recommended QLT, then trading at $20 on the Toronto Stock Exchange, as a buy.

A forecast takes into account a single scenario, such as: Things have been going well for QLT. Its lead product is going from strength to strength and its target market is ever expanding. Therefore, the stock will continue to do well and will increase in value. Buy.

Forecasts are usually wrong for one simple reason: nobody can predict the future. That's why sophisticated investors use scenarios rather than forecasts. Scenarios allow us to visualize a variety of possible futures, while forecasts envision only one. If a stock has performed poorly in the past, scenario thinking pushes us to visualize positive as well as negative futures. If a stock has performed well, scenario thinking leads us to consider possible future downsides.

Scenario thinking steers us away from the herd by forcing us to consider all the risks we have to contend with when we make an investment.

There is no one right scenario because we don't know what the future holds. But developing a set of scenarios spanning the range of possibilities gives the investor a sense of the upside and downside for a particular investment. On that basis, he can decide whether to invest and how much. Scenario thinkers, because they consider the contrarian view as well as the conventional one, are less likely than forecast thinkers to suffer major financial damage in investment bubbles like the technology stock boom of the 1990s.

In the case of QLT, the analyst's report made no mention of the major risk factor that most companies face: competition. Big mistake. Not long after the report was issued, U.S. drug giant Pfizer, along with Eyetech Pharmaceuticals, received approval in the U.S. for a competing macular degeneration treatment, Macugen. And in May 2005, Genentech, another U.S. company, announced that its macular degeneration entry, Lucentis, had been proven to improve patients' eyesight.

As a result, Visudyne's prospects dimmed considerably. To make matters still worse, QLT's diversification strategy proved disappointing. Shortly after Karen

Boodram's report was published, QLT acquired Atrix Laboratories, producer of Eligard, a drug to treat prostate cancer. But Eligard did not sell as well as anticipated and by July 2005, analysts were saying that QLT had overpaid for Atrix.

By November 2005, QLT's shares were trading at around $8, less than half of their value when they had been recommended as a buy ten months earlier.

By making a forecast that turned out to be wrong, Karen Boodram put herself in distinguished company. In 1929, just before the stock market crash that led to the Great Depression, Irving Fisher, a professor of economics at Yale University, said, "Stocks have reached what looks like a permanently high plateau."

Fisher's was just one of many recorded predictions by smart people that, in retrospect, seem ridiculous but at the time were taken seriously by other smart people. Early in the last century, a Daimler-Benz spokesman foresaw that there would never be more than 1,000 cars on Europe's roads because "that is the limit on the number of chauffeurs available." About the same time, in 1909, *Scientific American* assured its readers that "the automobile has practically reached the limit of its development." A few decades later, in 1979, *BusinessWeek* predicted that "with over 50 foreign cars already on sale here, the

Japanese auto industry isn't likely to carve out a big slice of the U.S. market."

Just like the financial forecasts that fill the pages of investment periodicals and Web sites today, these predictions about the automobile were credible because of the expertise of those making them. Similarly, no one could question the expertise of the Boeing engineer who, at the launch of the ten-passenger Boeing 247 in 1932, predicted, "There will never be a bigger plane built."

The Boeing engineer was no fool, even though his prediction sounds foolish more than seventy years later. The implications and future development of new technologies are notoriously hard to foresee even by the brainiest and best informed scientists. "There is not the slightest indication," said Albert Einstein in 1932, "that nuclear energy will ever be obtainable."

Because technological development is so unpredictable, investors putting their money on new technologies must be cautious. But caution does not mean being dismissive of all new products; pessimistic predictions are as likely to be wrong as optimistic ones. It was Thomas Watson, the chairman of IBM, who said in 1943, "I think there is a world market for maybe five computers." In 1977, Ken Olson, chairman of Digital Equipment, issued an equally wrong prediction. "There is," he said, "no reason anyone would want a computer in their home." As for Microsoft founder Bill Gates, his assessment in 1981 of the future of computer memory was as follows: "640K [kilobytes] ought to be enough for anybody."

A prediction can be optimistic and pessimistic at the same time and still be wrong. An example was Alexander Graham Bell's prophecy 125 years ago that "one day there will be a telephone in every major city in the U.S."

In assessing forecasts, the investor must consider the source. How objective is it? Does the forecaster have a stake in the success or failure of whatever product or technology he is talking about? While Bell had a stake in the success of the telephone, Darryl F. Zanuck, who ran Twentieth Century Fox, had a stake in the failure of television, which led him, in 1946, to state: "Television won't be able to hold onto any market it captures after the first six months. People will soon get tired of staring at a plywood box every night."

Only in retrospect does Zanuck's forecast for television's future seem absurd. In 1946, the Hollywood studio system was still powerful, movies dominated the entertainment industry, and most North Americans visited movie theatres at least weekly. Moreover,

Zanuck was right—watching a program on an early TV set with its small, fuzzy, black-and-white screen was a poor substitute for seeing big-name stars on larger-than-life screens in glorious Technicolor.

That there was a basis for Zanuck's forecast is evident in the staying power of movies sixty years later. Despite the advent of dazzling TV technology, a multitude of channels, and movies on DVD, theatrical films remain a multibillion-dollar industry. So while Zanuck's statement by itself was a bad forecast, it made good sense as one scenario to be considered among others.

How would a scenario thinker have approached the case of QLT when it was trading at $20? First, he or she would have listed the risk factors that might affect the company in the future:

1. The treatment might not work as well as hoped over the long term.
2. The company is small and may not have the financial clout necessary to compete internationally.
3. A competitor or competitors may develop other treatments for macular degeneration.
4. QLT is involved in a proposed merger with another drug company, and mergers can go wrong. (Karen Boodram's report

mentioned the pending merger but did
not identify it as a risk factor.)

5. At any given time, hundreds of small drug
developers are trying to strike it rich with
new treatments for previously incurable
diseases. Few succeed.

If we are looking at putting our money in QLT in 2004, competition is clearly the major risk. Even if a competitor's product isn't better, maybe having two or more competing treatments on the market will drive the price of Visudyne down to the point where QLT won't make any money. QLT's Visudyne may be better than the competition, yet the company would still find it difficult to compete against a drug behemoth such as Pfizer with its massive marketing presence. On the positive side, competition might help Visudyne by creating a bigger market for macular degeneration treatment.

The other big risk is the smallness of the company. Unlike a Pfizer or GlaxoSmithKline, everything has to click perfectly for QLT. A large company has dozens of drugs in its arsenal and won't suffer if one of them falls to new competition. QLT has other products as well, but it is dependent on Visudyne and that dependence is a major risk factor.

Would scenario thinking have prevented an investor from buying QLT at $20? Not necessarily. But the scenario thinker would have been less likely to make a big investment than an investor relying on an optimistic forecast that ignored or minimized the substantial downside. Investors who rely on advisors have a right to expect that the advisor will have examined all probable scenarios before recommending an investment. If a broker is recommending purchase of a certain stock, ask him to outline the various scenarios he has considered.

In the case of QLT, the scenario thinker, simply by applying common-sense thinking to a variety of possible futures, would soon realize that junior drug developers are a lot like junior mining companies trying to strike gold—risky, vulnerable businesses that must be approached with caution. That's the wonderful thing about getting into the habit of using scenarios: it forces us to think. And it shows us the questions we should be asking our investment advisors, questions that reveal whether the advisor is up to the job.

The QLT forecast was wrong for the same reason the forecasts of Thomas Watson and Bill Gates were wrong: they were all based on extrapolations of the present. Rather than envisioning a different future, these forecasters did what most people do—assume the future will be like the present, only a little bit more developed. And, in fact, this assumption is often correct. Boeing did not progress overnight from the ten-passenger 247 to today's 600-passenger 747. And it took several decades for the clunky, room-sized computing machines of Watson's day to morph into the sleek, high-powered laptops of today. Forecasters often fail to envision the transformative impact of continuous incremental improvements.

The herd instinct is another major cause of faulty forecasts. When everybody is saying that Bre-X's gold discovery in Busang, Indonesia, is the world's biggest and mutual fund managers are scooping up all the Bre-X shares they can get, it takes a brave contrarian to point out that no gold has yet been mined there and that perhaps the hype might be a touch exaggerated.

In the 1990s, thousands of small investors bought shares in Bre-X Minerals on the strength of enthusiastic forecasts by expert analysts employed by Canadian brokerage houses. Lawyers representing investors in a class-action suit against both the company and the brokers who promoted the stock said that without the expert forecasts, nobody would have bought the shares. The investors lost $6 billion when the mine turned out to contain no gold. Core samples from the site had been salted with real gold from elsewhere before being submitted for analysis. This was a case of outright fraud, and it worked brilliantly. Smart people bought the story and ignored any contrarian scenarios. They recommended the stock, with the result that vast sums of money were transferred from small investors to the Bre-X fraudsters.

"Nobody knows anything," was the famous assessment of the novelist and screenwriter William Goldman, commenting on the inability of Hollywood producers to predict which movies would become hits. Of course, he was exaggerating. Veteran producers have vast knowledge of filmmaking, just as the analysts who recommended Bre-X knew plenty about mining. But none of them can forecast accurately in all cases. Nobody can.

Scenario thinkers know this and therefore are always skeptical of forecasts. David Chapman, investment advisor for Union Securities, wrote the following in an article for *Investor's Digest* in May 2005: "With the growing demand for [uranium] ore and the need to find more, prices have only one place to go, and that is up." The scenario thinker instantly recognizes this statement, and all that resemble it, as laughable. By accepting such forecasts as gospel, millions of people have lost billions of dollars investing in gold at its peak or in stocks like Bre-X, Nortel, Enron, and so many others that had, according to some expert, "only one place to go, and that is up."

Chapman's prediction is based on the notion that, with conventional oil in short supply and world-wide energy demands soaring, hundreds of new nuclear plants are going to be built, and new supplies of uranium will be required. Like Darryl Zanuck's negative forecast for television, this is a sound thesis—as one possible scenario.

But there are other scenarios, too, and you needn't be an expert to find them. The economy moves in cycles; therefore, downturns and recessions are inevitable. When these happen, energy demand will likely decrease, and with it the price of uranium. There could be a political upheaval in China, whose supposedly "insatiable energy demands" are the basis for Chapman's forecast. Political instability could lead to economic chaos, and suddenly China's energy demands would be satisfied without 200 new nuclear reactors. Or a horrific replay of the Chernobyl disaster somewhere in the world could put a halt to new development of nuclear power plants everywhere.

A fundamental rule of scenario picking is as follows: when you look at your portfolio's performance under different scenarios, if all of the scenarios lead to beneficial results, then you either haven't thought of enough of them or the right ones. Go back and find some more. Look for all the things that could go wrong. There are always some.

HOW TO SPOT A SCENARIO

When a credible authority makes a comparison between current and past economic events, the chances are that he or she is offering a scenario risk-savvy investors should consider. In October, 2005, Alan Greenspan, chairman of the U.S. Federal Reserve Board, gave a speech in Tokyo to Japanese business leaders in which he discussed the rise in oil prices that had occurred during 2005, peaking in the wake of Hurricane Katrina.

"The effect of the current surge in oil prices . . . is likely to prove significantly less consequential to economic growth and inflation than the surge in the 1970s," he said. His reason was that the industrial economies have learned to use energy more efficiently. For example, the ratio of U.S. oil consumption to its gross domestic product has fallen by half since 1973.

The four-fold increase in oil prices imposed by the oil producing countries in 1973-74 raised price levels throughout the western economies while slowing economic growth. The result was a new economic phenomenon called "stagflation"—recession and inflation at the same time.

Greenspan was forecasting that the 2005 oil price spike will not trigger similar conditions. That's useful knowledge for investors—as long as they remember that, no matter how credible the source, a single forecast is only one of many possible futures.

Because the future is uncertain, any number of scenarios could occur. Scenario planning requires limiting that number to those that we consider most likely. For example, to state that interest rates will be 2.5 percent a year from now is a forecast whose chances of coming true are poor. But a statement proposing a high probability that the interest rate will range between 2 and 4 percent is a scenario set. As interest rates are usually adjusted in increments of a quarter-point (e.g., from 2 to 2.25), each quarter of a percentage point represents one scenario.

If we decide to accept this scenario set, the range of possible rates from 2 to 4 percent is what we are betting on, and any rates outside that range are ones we are betting against. Rather than trying to predict the future interest rate—an impossible task—we are choosing a range of probable rates and adjusting our portfolio accordingly. This makes risk manageable. If no rate in the 2- to 4-percent range is likely to cause us grief, then we have no problem. On the other hand, if we are okay at 2.5 percent but nearly bankrupt at 4 percent, we have to take steps to hedge against the possibility of 4 percent.

The challenge in formulating scenarios is to understand how far to go, both on the upside and downside. In this case, we ought not to be cavalier about dismissing rates outside the 2- to 4-percent range. A number outside that range—say, 6 percent might be unlikely but not unreasonable, in which case we should seriously consider including it as one of our scenarios.

What if one of the many scenarios we chose to bet against comes to pass and the interest rate jumps to 8 percent, causing us deep regret? Well, then we lose. But at least we considered the possibility of an 8 percent interest rate and made a rational decision to reject it. Many of the problems people experience as investors are a result of not knowing the bets they are making.

One way to formulate scenarios is to work backwards. You know that you are exposed to certain interest rates because you know what you own, whether it is interest-sensitive investments such as bonds or income trusts or, on the debit side, a mortgage or line of credit. Ask yourself this: What would interest rates have to be in order for my regret to be too high to bear? You may decide you are not going to accept losses of more than $100,000. What would interest rates have to be for such a loss to occur? If the answer is a highly improbable number, then you know you can proceed safely because any probable change in the interest rate is not going to cause major regret.

Using scenarios in this case doesn't force you to pick one right answer but rather to ask the question, "At what point would this risk factor hurt me?" If you knew that an increase of only half a percentage point would hurt you, then you would really have to worry about it. That's because if one-half of one percent would hurt, then 1 percent would kill—and a 1 percent move is always possible. Just by getting into the habit of thinking about likely and unlikely events, you become a more confident investor. You are not betting your savings on the opinions of one prominent guru or one advisor who, even with the best of intentions, may be totally wrong in his forecasts.

How might a scenario thinker approach the case of Google, the leading Internet search engine that became the hottest stock of 2004 and 2005? Google was first offered to the public in August 2004 at $85. Less than a year later, it was worth $300.

Should we buy the stock now, in the summer of 2005, on the assumption that Google's ascent is not yet over? Or should we avoid it on the assumption that any stock that has climbed so high so quickly may have run out of gas or be ready for a fall? If we listen to the Wall Street experts, there is no doubt about what we will do. Of thirty-two analysts surveyed in June 2005, twenty-five were rating Google a "buy" and seven called it a "hold," while none advocated selling. One of the analysts predicted Google would reach $360 within a year.

Wall Street wasn't always so positive. When the company first went public, the same analysts hugely underestimated how quickly its revenues and profits would grow and, as a result, their forecasts for the stock price were too conservative. They weren't even sure what Google was. Was it a technology company, as its leaders said, or was it an advertising company?

It is both. Its success is based on the technical excellence of its search engine. But Google's profitability depends on its efficiency as an advertising medium. Advertisers want to zero in on the customers who are most likely to be interested in their product. If you are selling, say, vitamin C, what better way to reach a customer than to have your ad pop up on the computer screen of an individual doing a Google search on vitamin C? Because of the popularity of this new, highly targeted form of advertising, Google's advertising revenues have surpassed those of the major TV networks as well as such newspaper companies as *The New York Times.*

Wall Street admires Google management's habit of always looking for new ways to make money; in 2005, for example, it was planning to introduce a video-viewing channel and an Internet payment system. The share price may seem high in terms of current earnings, but it's not so high if future estimated earnings are considered. That's why the analysts recommend buying or keeping the stock rather than selling it.

Of course, you can find naysayers if you look for them. One is John Hussman, manager of the Strategic Growth Fund, a U.S. mutual fund, who argues that Google is overvalued. In June 2005, he wrote as follows in his newsletter:

> The difficulty with Google isn't in the product. It's neat. It's hip. I use it almost daily. The real question is this—why do we assume that Google's revenues and earnings are going to grow exponentially from here? In a competitive

market, with few barriers to entry and no particular brand loyalty, an advertising company that's valued at one-fifth the market cap of General Electric is not likely to mount a secure defense for its revenue stream.

Unlike Microsoft, Adobe, or even Yahoo and Ebay, there's currently no benefit to users in aggregating around the same product as their "standard" and no high-cost obstacle to entry aside from smart statistical and computing algorithms. Therefore, there's no natural monopoly that would lead to a defensible competitive advantage. Sure, these guys are smart, and deliver useful, consumer oriented products. But when you value a company at 20 times revenues and over 100 times earnings, you're going to invite competition from some very, very intelligent people. What investors seem to be doing is paying an awful lot for future creativity. That might be reasonable, to at least some extent, if the company's dominant position in the industry had characteristics of a natural monopoly. But it doesn't. Usefulness of a product is insufficient for profitability unless it is coupled with scarcity.

Hussman makes a strong case that Google is vulnerable to competition and concludes it is worth

$40 at most. Meanwhile, a Wall Street expert forecasts it will rise to $360. We could flip a coin and choose one forecast over the other. Or, rather than rely on a single forecast, we could do some thinking for ourselves, create our own set of scenarios, and make our own decision based on whether, in our particular case, the upside of buying Google at $300 is greater than the downside.

In creating scenarios, it is useful, for this and other investment challenges, to look at similar cases that could be considered proxies for the case at hand. We don't do this under the assumption that the investment we are considering will simply repeat the history of some other investment, but as a way of coming up with a variety of scenarios that span different possibilities.

Google is a technology company that dominates a particular sector of retailing, that of Internet advertising. So proxies worth looking at would be Amazon.com and Nokia, two other technology companies that serve a mass market of consumers. Both, like Google, are dominant in their particular fields and both experienced spectacular rises in their stock prices.

Amazon is the leading Internet retailer, starting out as a bookseller and then expanding to music and other products. It was first issued to the public in

1997 at $1.50 a share and topped $100 at the peak of the Internet boom in 1999. The discussions as to whether such a price was justified at that time were eerily similar to those about Google in 2005. Amazon's proponents argued that, by leading the way into a new world of Internet retailing, the company stood to reap vast profits in the future and that its high valuation reflected those future profits.

Contrarians saw Amazon as a bubble that was sure to burst. The company wasn't making money, it had few assets, and its business model was unproven. Even Alan Greenspan, chairman of the U.S. Federal Reserve Board, weighed in to urge caution, calling the rapid rise in share values of Amazon and other Internet companies a case of "irrational exuberance."

As it turned out, the contrarians were right, but Amazon's advocates weren't totally wrong either. The Internet bubble burst in 2000 and took Amazon along with it. By the end of that year, its stock was worth about $15, an 86-percent drop from its 1999 peak. The people who bought at or near the top suffered devastating losses.

But those who supported the company as a valid business concept have turned out to be correct. Amazon has not only survived, but it has prospered. It sold almost $7 billion worth of stuff in 2004—not just books and music, but also such things as electronic equipment and beef ribs. The company is now profitable, and its stock in 2005 was in the mid-$30 range. Jeff Bezos, Amazon's founder, likes to point out that for a stock to go from $1.50 to around $35 in eight years is a good performance—which is true, but which is also small comfort to those who believed the "new paradigm" hype and bought Amazon at its top. They would have done just as well by investing the same amount in beer because the deposits on the empty bottles would have been worth as much as their stock which, at one point, dipped under $10. At least they'd have enjoyed the beer.

Nokia, the Finnish cellphone manufacturer, has more in common with Google than Amazon in that, like Google, it was profitable when its stock reached for the stars. Between 1994 and 1999, Nokia shares on the New York Stock Exchange increased in value twentyfold.

Like Google, Nokia is an innovative, well-managed company. But it has a longer history than Google, and that history reveals that even good companies stumble sometimes, a fact of life that Google investors might do well to remember. Nokia has strong competition from such companies as Motorola, Samsung, and LG. These and other competitors came out with new phone designs that ate into Nokia's market share, resulting in disappointing earnings. In 2002, the stock price tumbled, although not as drastically as Amazon's. But things turned around for Nokia in 2004, and by the summer of 2005 some analysts were saying the stock looked like a bargain.

What these two examples tell us is that good companies can be both overvalued and undervalued at different times. The stock market does not always behave rationally, although eventually it manages to evaluate most companies appropriately. The Amazon and Nokia examples also tell us that investors get skittish with stocks that have risen spectacularly. As it did with Nokia, the market is likely to punish Google for any major misstep.

On the other hand, Google's achievement in overtaking major newspapers and TV networks in advertising revenue is stunning, and the company is in the enviable position of being the leader in a rapidly growing market. One scenario sees spending on U.S. online marketing and advertising growing from $14.7 billion to $26 billion between 2005 and 2010.

To buy Google or not to buy Google? No single answer applies to everyone, because each investor has unique goals and an individual degree of risk-tolerance. The first thing to do is establish our benchmark. Are we buying Google because we expect it will enjoy another $200 jump in value? In that case, our benchmark is $500 and we will suffer regret if the stock does not attain that value. (The key concepts of benchmarks and regret will be explored in detail in the next chapter.) If $500 is our benchmark and our scenario analysis indicates the stock is unlikely to reach it, we should not buy.

Perhaps our benchmark is less ambitious—such as that the stock will maintain its current value in relation to its earnings. In that case, an increase of 10 percent a year would probably meet our expectations. Under this scenario, if we hold the stock for several years, we stand to make a substantial gain.

One we have established a benchmark, we need to assess the risks to which Google is exposed:

1. Competition risk. Google is vulnerable to competition, from big names like Yahoo! and Microsoft to some brash new contender that could appear, like Google, out of nowhere.
2. Technology risk. Google's technology was much superior to its rivals when it started out, explaining its rapid rise to prominence. The rivals have caught up now, and Google will have to fight hard to increase its revenues.

3. Economy risk. An economic downturn could decrease revenues and profits.
4. Management risk. All companies goof up sometimes, and Google's turn may come soon. Will management be as innovative and effective now that Google is a major company as it was when it was an upstart?

The upside is a mirror image of the downside:

1. Competition may not hurt Google. Amazon has plenty of competition and, rather than hurt the market leader, competition appears to have helped it by increasing the popularity of Internet shopping.
2. Google's technology has been a strength since the company was launched, and it's reasonable to assume it can continue to build on that solid foundation.
3. An economic downturn might not hurt Internet advertising as much as other media. Users are already paying for their connection, so they will continue to use the 'net even in hard times. Also, advertisers trying to cut costs may find the Internet a more cost-effective place to put their message than print or broad-cast media.

4. Nothing indicates that Google's management has grown sloppy or complacent.

It is reasonable to conclude that, at a price of $300, the upside in Google stock is less—and the downside greater—than when it was offered to the public at $85. This does not necessarily mean that, in the case of each individual investor, the upside is less than the downside. A rational investor may well choose a scenario set that would see the stock trade in a range between $200 and $500. In that case, the upside is twice the downside. An equally rational investor might come to a less optimistic conclusion. Which scenario is the right one? That is entirely up to you, the investor.

One of the determinants of your decision will be your assessment of how much regret you will experience should the investment not work out as you had hoped. How patient an investor are you? Would you be content to hold Google for a few years and sell for a $50-per-share profit? Would a modest profit be sufficient, given the risk these shares entail?

As we will see in the next chapter, most people regret losing what they have more than they regret not getting what they don't have. In other words, buying 100 shares of Google, at a cost of $30,000, and losing half of it should Google decline to $150, would be worse than not buying the shares and watching Google rise to $450. In either case, we don't have $15,000 that we would have had but the regret of losing is greater than the regret of not winning. This is a matter of personal psychology that has nothing to do with an objective analysis of Google and its future. Nevertheless, it is important to recognize that the potential for regret enlarges the downside at the expense of the upside.

Should you decide to buy Google, you then have the question of *how much* to buy. A good way to approach this question is to determine the limits you want to place on your losses should your worst-case scenario come to pass. You might decide to choose John Hussman's analysis as your worst-case scenario: Google plunges to $30, a 90-percent drop. How much money can you accept losing should that occur? The answer to that question determines how much you should buy.

If we were also considering buying IBM at the same time, we might come to a different conclusion because the worst-case scenario for IBM is unlikely to be a 90-percent drop. So you might buy more IBM, even though you think its upside is less compelling than Google's. Do this loss-limiting exercise before making any investment. And if your worst-case scenario doesn't show any losses, you need a worse worst-case scenario, because there are no sure things in the world of investment.

Another hot investment in 2005 was not an individual stock, but a country: India. Assumed until recently to be part of the impoverished Third World, India is now increasingly viewed as an economic powerhouse in the making—and a glittering investment opportunity. But just as with any other potential investment, whether it be uranium or Google, we need to approach a region as scenario thinkers, not forecasters.

In all our scenario planning, we should keep in mind the upside bias of the financial media. Financial editors are looking for good stories, and a story depicting a fabulous surge of prosperity for India is a better story than one explaining the pitfalls facing the country. This is understandable because India's downside is not news; India rising is news.

Another factor in the upside bias is that many of the media's sources are executives of companies or sellers of financial products. It is normal that they would play up the good news about their company or mutual fund and downplay the bad. Although reporters and editors try to be fair and objective, an upside bias inevitably creeps into much of what gets published. We can usually count on the media, therefore, to provide us with the positive scenarios. In order to have a balanced assessment, we will need to come up with the downside ones ourselves.

The major upside factor is India's people. Desperate to escape poverty, they are prepared to work harder than affluent Europeans and North Americans who have never known it. Thomas Friedman wrote in *The New York Times* that, while the French in 2005 were voting to retain their thirty-five-hour work week, upwardly mobile Indian workers, if they could, would work thirty-five-hour *days*. "They are answering our telephones but will soon be designing our computers and airplanes," he observed.

Friedman was referring to the phenomenon of outsourcing, or "offshoring," through which millions of jobs have been moved from wealthy countries to developing countries where they can be done more cheaply. So, when Canadians have problems with their computers, their calls are often handled by technicians in India.

Previously, outsourcing was restricted to manufacturing jobs—making electronic equipment or running shoes, for example—and back-office jobs such as call centres. Now communications technology is allowing highly skilled jobs once thought non-exportable to be moved to India as well. Arjun Kalyanpur, a radiologist, occupies one of them. After working as an emergency-room radiologist in the U.S., he decided in 1999 to return home to India. But he still works, in effect, in the U.S., reading images e-mailed to him by emergency-room nightshifts. He is paid about as much as he would have earned had he remained physically in North America and, because of the time difference, he has the advantage of working during the Indian day rather than overnight as when he lived in the U.S.

India's high standards of education are a critical factor in its economic success. Author Suketu Mehta arrived in New York City from Bombay at the age of fourteen. At his Bombay school, mathematics had been his worst subject, and he ranked near the bottom of his class. In New York, to both his own and his parents' amazement, he ranked near the top—as he did in American history. "If I were now to move with my family to India, my children—who go to one of the best private schools in New York—would have to take remedial math and science courses to get into a good school in Bombay," he wrote in *The New York Times*.

Good education would not have helped without the economic and political liberalization that has taken place in India over the past fifteen years. Many restrictions on foreign investment were lifted and the political system has become more stable and democratic. As a result, capital is pouring into India—about U.S.$8 billion in 2005 alone. Economic growth in the same year was expected to be around 7 percent, making India one of the world's fastest-growing economies.

In May 2005, Report on Business Television interviewed Bhim Asdhir, president and CEO of Excel Fund Management, whose Excel India Fund, which Asdhir manages, is a convenient way for Canadians to invest in India. "Every time I go to India I am amazed with the wealth," he said, pointing out that around 30 million or 40 million Indians are escaping poverty and joining the middle class every year. "You see scooters, motorcycles, cars, TVs, people going out, eating out. . . . There is a lot of wealth in the hands of people."

A dramatic example of progress is the use of cellphones, up from about 1 million in 2000 to 50 million in 2005 and projected to grow to 200 million by 2008, according to Asdhir. Cellphones are another way in which modern communications, developed by the industrialized countries, are helping the developing world to advance economically. A modern economy cannot function without efficient communications. Putting a cellphone in everyone's pocket is cheaper and faster than wiring the whole country for conventional phone service.

India, because of its high fertility rate (2.78 children per woman, compared to 1.72 in China and 1.61 in Canada) has one of the world's youngest populations, with more than 54 percent under the age of twenty-five. Some analysts see this as an important asset, providing the country with a large and steady supply of productive workers to build its economy as well as a large cohort of eager consumers.

Most articles on India make only passing reference to the downside. But before we consider investing in this remarkable country, we need to look at some of the risks:

1. Currency risk. The Indian rupee is vulnerable to any serious economic uncertainty, such as a political upheaval in Saudi Arabia that would disrupt oil production or a global recession. In times of uncertainty, investors head for safe havens, and India doesn't qualify. Many investors would pull their money out. Consequently, the rupee, and along with it the value of Indian investments, would fall.

2. Infrastructure risk. A modern economy requires a vast physical infrastructure of

telecommunications, roads, airports, public transit, port facilities, communications, water, sewage, and garbage disposal. India's rapid population growth means that its infrastructure needs are all but impossible to satisfy. The need for massive public works construction creates opportunities for investors in India, but at the same time the infrastructure shortfall may increasingly act as a brake on economic growth.

3. Energy risk. India relies on coal, one of the dirtiest fuels, for 80 percent of its electricity needs. It is exempt from the Kyoto agreement, but that exemption could be lifted in some future global pact, in which case India might have to reduce its dependence on coal. In the meantime, it can't mine enough to keep up with the demand, even though it has large reserves. The state monopoly, Coal India, is inefficient and lacks money to develop new mines. India also imports coal, but crumbling ports and poor rail facilities hamper deliveries.

4. Geopolitical risk. India and neighbouring Pakistan have a history of hostile relations and both are armed with nuclear weapons.

5. AIDS. News articles lauding India as the next Asian economic tiger routinely fail to mention that HIV/AIDS is rampaging across the country. According to government estimates, India has 5.1 million cases of HIV/AIDS, which would make it the second most afflicted country after South Africa, which has 5.3 million cases. But Richard Feachem, executive director of the Global Fund to Fight AIDS, rejects the 5.1 million figure as too low, as do other AIDS experts. "India is in first place," Feacham told *The Toronto Star* in 2005. India "is or is becoming the global epicentre for the pandemic." Inadequate health care and the failure of the government to educate the public about prevention have allowed HIV/AIDS to gain a foothold. Indian pharmaceutical companies produce high quality anti-AIDS drugs but they are not getting to the people who need them. Ashoik Alexander, head of Avahan, an organization to combat HIV/AIDS established in India by the Gates Foundation, warns that the epidemic is growing explosively in parts of the country. The result could be social disaster and

economic upheaval—a tragedy for India and a financial blow to investors who put too much credence in glowing reports that ignore the dark side.

Just as with Google, in the case of India we can use proxies to help us develop a comprehensive set of scenarios. The proxies are other big countries that have attempted the transition from underdeveloped to developed. Japan, Mexico, and Argentina are three we might look at because each has experienced economic development differently. Each embarked on the road to modernization with, like India, large populations, large problems, and large potential.

Japan has succeeded brilliantly and become one of the world's economic powerhouses; Mexico has had mixed results; and Argentina is a failure because of bad government, economic mismanagement, and overreliance on resources. So we can consider the recent economic histories of these countries as the basis for three probable scenarios for India. Looking at India's future through this perspective should enable us to make a more realistic assessment than if we rely completely on glib forecasts in the financial press that gloss over the downside.

India's biggest economic advantage over the three proxies is that, having been ruled as part of the

British Empire, its people speak English, the language of international business and of the U.S., the world's only superpower. That's why call centres serving anglophones are in India rather than China, another emerging economy with plenty of cheap labour. Many other activities, from data processing to the editing of scientific papers, have been outsourced to take advantage of India's low-cost, high-quality, English-speaking labour. This kind of economic activity has the advantage of low capital costs because no expensive production facilities are required.

Added to this advantage are two positive characteristics India shares with Japan: one is relative political stability and democratic government; the other is an emphasis on developing human capital through education. Japan still has its forestry and fishing industries but it is brainpower, as exhibited in the relentless product enhancement practised by its automotive and electronics industries, that has made it an international economic star. Similarly, India's education system has created the "raw materials"—educated brains—that have allowed it to excel in such fields as computer technology and pharmaceuticals.

On the other hand, India resembles the Latin American proxies, not Japan, in the deep social divisions that afflict its society. And in its high birth rate, it resembles Mexico, while again it is Japan's opposite.

Some observers see India's expanding, youthful population as an asset, but this seems at odds with experience elsewhere: the poorest countries in the world are also the youngest. A high proportion of young people is expensive because of the cost of educating them. And there is also the challenge of creating employment. Young people who have no useful outlet for their energies are always a disruptive force. A large labour pool is good thing but it is a law of nature that too much of a good thing is a bad thing.

The prospective India investor might come to the conclusion that the country has an upside that is bigger than those of more developed countries such as the U.S. or Great Britain. He might also sensibly conclude that the downside scenario is similarly greater than those of the U.S. and Great Britain. Because the downside scenarios in India are more extreme, the investor would manage his Indian risk by having fewer eggs in his Indian basket than in his British or American baskets. If India continues to prosper, he might regret not buying more Indian eggs, but that decision can be justified as insurance against the bigger downside.

Emerging markets are always characterized by volatility, and India is no exception—as demonstrated by the returns of the Excel India Fund. If you had put money into this fund in 2000, your annual returns as of April 30, 2005, would have been 1.19 percent, or less than a risk-free bank deposit. On the other hand, if you had invested in 2003, your annual return to 2005 would have been a robust 30.33 percent. There are much more cost-efficient ways to invest in India than this fund, which has an outsized management expense ratio (MER) of 3.89 percent. The shares of some Indian banks, which can be expected to benefit from the surge in consumer borrowing from the country's expanding middle class, are traded on the New York Stock Exchange. So are those of other Indian companies such as Infosys Technologies, one of the Excel Fund's top holdings. Of course, you pay no management fee to hold shares directly.

A savvy investor understands that risk is an essential part of investing; it is something to be managed, not feared. He also understands that the only certainty about the future is that it will differ from the past. Both of these principles might lead to the conclusion that investing in India makes sense. But even investors who decide that India's upside greatly outweighs its downside must monitor their India investments vigilantly. Our spectacular success proxy, Japan, suffered a stock market crash in 1989 from which it has yet to recover fully. Investors who were unlucky in their timing lost badly. Japan proved not to be a "buy-and-hold" investment, and neither is

India. The investor who decides India is a risk worth taking should understand that managing Indian risk will require being prepared to bail out quickly.

The smartest people in the world, people like Albert Einstein and Alexander Graham Bell, made forecasts that were wrong because they extrapolated from the present. It would seem to be human nature to do this—which might explain why the herd instinct so often takes over as the investing masses stampede in the same direction at the same time.

It happened during the 1990s, when some people took out mortgages on their houses in order to have more money to invest in Internet stocks. These stocks, so the story went, had nowhere to go but up because they represented a "new paradigm," meaning that the Internet was a new way of doing business whose potential was unlimited. As it turned out, there was one other direction in which these stocks could move—down. In retrospect, what those aggressive Internet investors did seems mad, but at the time it made perfect sense to large numbers of people.

In 2005, oil is also supposed to be the beneficiary of a "new paradigm" because the world is running out of it just when demand, because of the explosive economic growth of China and India, is soaring. So, instead of moving in its historical cyclical fashion, the price of oil, because of the new paradigm, has only one place to go: up.

Both the Internet and oil are examples of forecast thinking as opposed to scenario thinking. What the herd doesn't understand is that the "new paradigm" is only one scenario. Obviously, there are others, including one that says the old paradigm may have life in it yet. Investing in the energy industry may well be a wise move, but only if we have thought it through first, understand the risks we are taking, and have a plan to ensure that those risks are manageable.

First, we have to decide which energy scenarios we are going to bet on and which we are going to bet against. This is a tough one because there are strong arguments for the different points of view. Deborah Yedlin explained the issue well in an article in *The Globe and Mail* in June 2005: "The question is whether current pricing is truly a reflection of market fundamentals—and concern supply just won't be enough to meet demand—or if it is simply a case of irrational exuberance in the energy world."

So we have two basic scenarios. The first says that lofty stock prices are justified because current high energy prices are permanent and, if anything, likely to rise further. The other says that the energy sector, like the Internet several years ago, is a bubble ready to burst. Of course, there is an endless supply of alternate scenarios. Maybe the price of oil will stabilize somewhere between $50 and $60 a barrel, and the price of energy stocks will stabilize as well. Or maybe political turmoil in Saudi Arabia, Iran, or Venezuela will create a severe shortage, leading to prices of $200 a barrel. Or maybe an oil shortage won't lead to a sharp spike in prices because it will trigger a world recession, thereby putting the brakes on economic activity and dampening demand. Or maybe someone will find a way to produce an alternative fuel cheaply enough to make a major dent in demand for oil and natural gas.

Let's look a bit closer at the two basic scenarios. The basis of the position of the "oil bulls" is that the world is running out of lower-cost conventional oil supplies at a time when demand has never been greater. Jeffrey Rubin, chief economist for CIBC World Markets and a prominent oil bull, is forecasting an average oil price of US$77 a barrel (about $14 more than the price in September 2005) over the next five years. By 2010, he expects oil to trade as high as $100 a barrel.

Rubin bases his view on the work of M. King Hubbert, an American geophysicist, author of the Hubbert curve, a theory of oil depletion. Most of the world's largest oil fields are beyond their production peaks, according to Hubbert. The members of the Organization of Petroleum Exporting Countries (OPEC) no longer have much spare capacity, and Rubin's projections show additions to gross world oil supply falling off sharply beginning in 2006. "Obviously," he wrote in an April 2005 report, "prices will have to rise to keep demand within the available supply constraint."

The London-based Oil Depletion Analysis Centre (ODAC) concurs. Within two years, it said in a 2005 report, new projects coming on stream will be insufficient to offset global oilfield declines. The only way to balance supply and demand will be through steep price increases or conservation.

Reining in demand will be no easy task. The two largest countries in the world, China and India, are emerging industrial giants with an exploding demand for energy. There has been a massive movement of industrial production to such low-wage countries, which are less energy efficient than the wealthy countries. As Chinese incomes rise, so does individual energy consumption. As a result, world demand for crude oil grew by 3.4 percent in 2004, the most in thirty years and three times the average growth of the past twenty-five years. Yet by the end of the year, per-capita oil consumption in China was still merely an eighth that of South Korea.

Clearly, Chinese demand has a long way to go. Even in the U.S., per-capita consumption was continuing to rise. Americans were driving more than ever and living in bigger homes. These trends more than offset improvements in energy efficiency.

Even if demand were to drop, oil prices might not necessarily follow in the same direction. The energy market has become less responsive to supply and demand in recent years and more at the mercy of speculators and hedge funds whose bets are not always based on rational considerations. Another factor complicating the outlook for oil stocks is that some companies won't get the full market price for the oil they have in the ground because they have hedged by selling future production forward at prices lower than the current market.

The price of a barrel of oil dropped below US$25 in late September 2001, but by July 2005 it was hovering around $60 and it briefly topped $70 after Hurricane Katrina struck the Gulf coast of the U.S. Rubin is not the only one predicting more expensive oil. Goldman Sachs, a well-respected U.S. investment house, issued a report saying the oil price could spike as high as $105 a barrel.

In 2004, oil and gas shares were the best-performing industry group on the Toronto Stock Exchange. In fact, the iUnits capped energy index, an exchange-traded fund (ETF) comprising the energy companies on the Toronto Stock Exchange, was the best-performing ETF in the world, with a one-year return to July 2005 of 73.6 percent.

If we believe Jeffrey Rubin, the sector has a bright future. Energy stock valuations, he predicts, "should follow a similar trajectory to the one they charted in the 1970s. Between 1973 and 1979, the oil and gas index of the (Toronto Stock Exchange) more than doubled."

The energy bulls reject any comparison between the state of the energy industry in the summer of 2005 and that of the Internet industry before that bubble burst. Unlike Amazon and other Internet stocks, the oil companies are raking in profits and carry little debt. As well, the higher stock values are fully justified by the higher earnings the energy companies are enjoying. This means that, even though energy stocks have soared, they are not expensive. For example, in June 2005, EnCana, a major natural gas company, traded at only 9.5 times its estimated earnings for 2006, a low multiple, while Google's price-to-earnings ratio was 44. Those numbers suggest that Google is an expensive stock, while EnCana is still moderately priced.

The bullish argument is a powerful one and is fast becoming the conventional wisdom, which is a good reason to treat it with suspicion. The scenario thinker never allows herself to be swept away by majority opinion. When the herd is rushing in one direction, she looks for contrarian scenarios that point elsewhere. The trouble with conventional scenarios is that they are all from inside the same box. You need ideas from outside the box.

Sometimes you can find them in surprising places. Geoff MacDonald manages one of the more successful Canadian mutual funds, Trimark Canadian Endeavour. He has $2 billion to invest, and none of it, as of the summer of 2005, was in energy. MacDonald has excellent contrarian credentials—unlike many fund managers, he did not have Nortel Networks and Bombardier in his fund's portfolio when both plunged in value. In 2005, he doesn't have energy stocks because he doesn't believe the high prices will last. "High prices always kill prices," he told *The Globe and Mail.* They will spur companies to develop more energy sources and consumers to conserve. Yet oil-company stocks are trading at prices that assume the per-barrel price can only increase. And that makes them too risky.

A danger signal is that the resource sector has made money for six years running. Can this continue? Only if one believes that a new paradigm has banished the cyclical behaviour that has always characterized that sector. Like MacDonald, the International Energy Agency forecasts that high prices will result in declining demand—which, both history and logic tell us, will push down the share prices of energy suppliers. Other skeptics point to the likelihood of an economic slowdown in China and to increased oil stockpiles in the U.S. as helping to keep the lid on prices. So, while energy stocks aren't likely to crash the way Internet stocks did in 1999, they may not have a lot higher to climb. We may be due for a small correction or a period of stability, which means investing in energy in the summer of 2005 isn't going to make us much money.

There is no correct scenario for energy prices, because the future is unknown and unknowable. But in this case, unlike that of a small company like QLT, a wide range of off-the-shelf scenarios is readily available. Energy prices are one of the central issues of our times, so deep thinkers such as those mentioned above have written about it extensively. You can assemble your energy scenarios simply by searching for them in publications that offer well-researched articles on business and international politics. But make sure you include the contrarians, even those with extreme views.

Once you have selected a range of possible futures to consider, you may feel yourself pressured to choose one. Not only do you not have to do that—you should not. Choosing one scenario is forecast thinking, not scenario thinking. Because there is no such thing as a right scenario before the fact, there is no point in choosing one.

The purpose of assembling a set of scenarios is to provide a solid understanding of the upside and downside. If you conclude that the upside for energy prices is less than the downside, then don't make an investment in energy because, on a risk-adjusted basis, it's a bad bet. If the upside is bigger than the downside, then go for it. But don't forget to do the loss-limiting exercise explained above. The risk-savvy investor makes no investments that could lead to unacceptable losses under the worst-case scenario.

In June, 2003, a major Swiss bank, Credit Suisse, became one of the first banks to sign on to the Equator Principles, a set of environmentally friendly guidelines to be applied in making loans to major development projects.

Banks often have been attacked for financing mines, dams, and other projects that damage both the environment and local populations. In response, the International Finance Corp., an arm of the World Bank, developed the Equator Principles, which it described as a "voluntary set of guidelines for managing environmental and social issues in project finance lending." The principles apply to all projects costing US$50 million or more. A long list of major banks, including Canada's Royal Bank, Scotiabank, and Canadian Imperial Bank of Commerce, have signed on.

At first glance, this seems like an odd move. Why would a bank pledge to follow environmental guidelines in its lending policies? Shouldn't its managers be tending to the bottom line rather than taking up trendy causes?

Actually, signing on to the Equator Principles was straightforward business management, explained Bernd Schanzenbacher of Credit Suisse First Boston, Credit Suisse's investment bank. By adopting the principles, Credit Suisse reduces its risk of being sued because of damage caused by projects it funds.

"Environmental risk is business risk, it's as simple as that," Schanzenbacher said. "So our ignorance of environmental risks can lead to costly litigation, but it can also lead to negative publicity and even revenue reduction."

If banks are taking steps to protect themselves from environmental risk, then perhaps individual investors should be doing the same. The biggest environmental risk is climate change and it would be foolhardy not to take into account the scenario that says it is causing major damage to the planet, and that this damage will worsen in the future. Even if the investor believes the threat to be overblown or non-existent, he might prefer, for his own financial health, to own shares in green companies rather than dirty ones whose future may be precarious.

As an example of what the future may hold for such companies, in 2004, lawyers representing eight American states sued the U.S.'s largest utilities, demanding that they reduce emissions of "green-house" gases. "Global warming threatens our health, our economy, our natural resources, and our children's future," said New York Attorney-General Eliot Spitzer. "It is clear we must act."

Carbon dioxide levels have risen to 370 parts per million (ppm) after being less than 290 ppm for hundreds of thousands of years. Without action to curb emissions, scientists fear that atmospheric carbon could be as high as 1,000 ppm by the end of the century. They warn that carbon dioxide and other greenhouse gases trap heat in the atmosphere, thereby changing global weather patterns and causing higher sea levels, drought, and loss of farmland.

Because the future is unknowable, we can't know exactly what will happen because of climate change. But we do know that the climate is already changing.

In the past 100 years, world temperatures have risen by 0.6 degrees. While that may not seem like much, small increases in average temperatures can have a big impact; during the last ice age the Earth was just 5 to 9 degrees cooler. According to the U.S. National Centre for Atmospheric Research, nine of the ten warmest years on record have occurred in the last decade. Ice is retreating in the Arctic and glaciers are melting all over the world.

A majority of scientists who have studied it believe climate change is a result of human activity, namely the release of greenhouse gases into the atmosphere. In 1995, some 2,000 scientists and government officials backed a report known as the Intergovernmental Panel on Climate Change (IPCC). Based on 133 scientific publications, it said the evidence points to "a discernible human influence on global climate." The IPCC findings were the basis for the Kyoto Protocol under which countries representing half the global economy committed themselves to reducing emissions.

However, it is a fundamental tenet of this book that investors should consider a variety of future scenarios rather than cling to one forecast, no matter how probable that forecast might seem to them. In this respect, it is important to note that not every scientist agrees with the IPCC.

One of the most outspoken sceptics is Fred Singer, a former Princeton University physicist and former director of the U.S. Weather Satellite Service. In a letter to Canadian media in 2005, he wrote: "Climate science research is rapidly moving away from the hypothesis that the human release of greenhouse gases, specifically CO_2, is in any way significantly contributing to global climate change."

Jan Veizer, a University of Ottawa geologist, also downplays the importance of carbon emissions in climate change. He believes celestial phenomena such as solar radiation set off climate change which may, however, be amplified by greenhouse gas emissions.

Richard Lindzen, professor of meteorology at the Massachusetts Institute of Technology, is another contrarian. "As a scientist, I can find no substantive basis for the warming scenarios being popularly described," he writes. "Moreover, according to many studies I have read by economists, agronomists, and hydrologists, there would be little difficulty adapting to such warming if it were to occur."

For every doubter, however, there are several who argue that cutting carbon emissions is both essential and urgent. "The science is done," says Andrew Weaver, a University of Victoria climatologist. Some may dismiss climate change research as "junk science," he told CBC, but at the same time industry is developing cleaner energy alternatives, just as it did for ozone-depleting CFCs in the 1990s. "It's junk science while there are no widgets," said Weaver. "Suddenly it's true once they have a widget." He is optimistic that industry, rather than governments, will take the lead in developing clean sources of energy.

From the investor's point of view, global warming is a risk regardless of whether one considers it a serious threat or not. A 10 percent chance of calamity would motivate an individual or business to take out insurance, points out Stephen Schneider, a Stanford University climatologist. So even if the investor calculates there is only a 10 per cent chance of climate change causing severe consequences, she would be well-advised to hedge against it.

Moreover, as Weaver points out, climate change brings opportunities as well as risks, a fact Pat Broe understands well. He is the Denver entrepreneur who in 1997 bought the rundown Hudson Bay port of Churchill, Manitoba, from the Canadian federal government for the nominal sum of $10. As the Arctic ice retreats, Arctic shipping lanes shorter by thousands of miles than more southerly routes will be available for longer periods. As a result, Broe told the *New York Times*, he expects the Churchill port could bring in $100 million a year.

Few investors have an opportunity to buy a Hudson Bay port. But they have a multitude of opportunities to invest in companies that are committed to green technologies. Once the only such companies were small, underfunded, risky startups. Now the ranks of green companies include such industrial giants as General Electric and Toyota.

In May, 2005, General Electric pledged to double its research spending on clean technology from $700 million a year to $1.5 billion by 2010. Jeffrey Immelt, the company's chairman, said GE also plans to increase its revenues from environmentally friendly technologies to $20 billion by that date. By 2015, half of the company's sales are expected to come from such products. In other words, GE is going green not for public relations reasons but for business reasons.

"We think green means green," Immelt told *U.S. News and World Report*. "This is a time period where environmental improvement is going to lead toward profitability. This is not a hobby to make people feel good."

The technologies GE is developing include wind power generation, advanced water treatment systems, and more energy-efficient appliances, airplanes, and locomotives. The company wants the U.S. government to enact laws to curb greenhouse gas emissions, thereby creating more demand for GE technologies in wind and nuclear power, natural gas turbines, and coal gasification.

Even without government action, rising energy prices are favouring companies that can provide energy efficient products. Every exhibitor at the Tokyo Auto Show, in October 2005, was showing off new energy efficient vehicles using electric batteries and hydrogen fuel cells. Larry Burns, General Motors's vice-president of research and development, told an Associated Press reporter at the show that GM's fuel cell system will be competitive with gasoline engines in performance by 2010.

Some may have problems seeing General Motors as "green." But the carmakers, out of self-interest, have bought into the need for emissions reductions. Other companies, such as the oil giant Exxon Mobil, have not. Under the leadership of chairman Lee Raymond, it favours the scenario that sees fossil fuels continuing to power the world's economies rather than the one that sees them eventually being supplanted by cleaner technologies.

Exxon disputes the idea that fossil fuels are the main cause of climate change, supports the U.S. government's decision not to sign the Kyoto Accord, opposes capping greenhouse gas emissions, and is a generous supporter of research organizations that agree with its position.

Does all of this make Exxon a bad investment? Not so far. It is the largest and most profitable oil company in the world. The issue for investors is whether its stance on global warming makes it a riskier investment going forward than some of its competitors in the energy business who are diversifying into alternatives to fossil fuels.

Andrew Logan, program manager of Ceres, a Boston-based partnership between environmental groups and institutional investors, believes it does. "There are two possible scenarios," he told the *Wall Street Journal* in June, 2005. In one scenario, the majority of scientists who believe global warming is an established fact turn out to be wrong. As a result, "there's no climate change in which case Exxon will do well. But if the scientists are correct and we have to find a way to transform the way we use energy, then Exxon is going to lag significantly behind its competitors."

These competitors include Royal Dutch/Shell Group which has spent $1.5 billion since 1999 on renewable energy, mainly solar and wind power. BP has spent $530 million on solar and wind. Exxon, meanwhile, is supporting a project at Stanford University to, among other things, find ways to reduce the cost of renewable energy. But it is spending only $100 million over the next 10 years, a fraction of what Shell has already spent building a business in alternative energy. Shell says its wind business is already turning a profit.

A carriage manufacturer who decided to diversify his product line when the first automobiles arrived on the scene had a greater upside and smaller downside than one who stubbornly clung to the belief that the automobile was a fad that couldn't possibly last. Similarly, an energy company that clings stubbornly to fossil fuels runs the danger of becoming a fossil itself.

The investor who wants to protect his portfolio against environmental risk has many tools at his disposal. One is the Carbon Disclosure Project, a London-based organization formed to foster collaboration among institutional investors regarding climate change. It issues reports that identify which investments carry the greatest environmental risks. For example, some banks have more than half of their commercial loans in sectors exposed to both regulatory and weather risks of climate change.

As always, the investor has to balance risk and reward. These banks might be highly profitable because they are able to charge their risk-exposed borrowers more for loans than less risky customers would have to pay. But that profitability might be short-lived if climate-related problems leave the banks with too many non-performing loans on their books.

As the 2005 Carbon Disclosure report makes clear, the stakes are high: "Taking climate risks into account is now becoming part of smart financial management. Failure to do so may well be tantamount to an abdication of fiduciary responsibility and indication of poor management."

Such poor management may leave a company exposed to lawsuits similar to those against asbestos and tobacco companies. On the other hand, a company that manages its environment risk well stands to benefit from emissions trading markets, such as the European Union Greenhouse Gas Emissions Trading Scheme (EU ETS), that allow clean companies to sell emission "credits" to dirty ones. At the same time, it can save itself major amounts of money by becoming more efficient. For example, in 1995, Dow Chemical set itself the goal of reducing energy use per pound of production by 20 per cent by 2005. Since then, it has saved U.S.$3 billion in energy costs.

Scenario planning is a fascinating exercise that ranges in scope from the very small (a junior drug company like QLT) to the immense – in the case of climate change, the very future of the planet. As in the other examples, it is up to the individual investor to decide which scenarios to protect herself against and which to bet against. The course of action she chooses will depend on various factors, including her risk tolerance and time horizon. As always, the investor should not forget to apply the loss-limiting exercise in which she determines how great a loss she could accept should the worst-case scenario come to pass.

Peter Schwartz, a well-known American management consultant, is a big believer in scenarios. "If you try to predict something, you end up with very conventional ideas," he says. "Scenarios help you anticipate surprises."

That's another way of saying that pushing yourself to think of multiple scenarios automatically guides you towards out-of-the-box thinking. In Chapter 1, we described how Robert Rubin, as president of investment house Goldman Sachs, took precautions against the almost unthinkable possibility that the U.S. government would default on some of its credit obligations. "In theory, you don't ever want to be in a position where even a remote risk can hurt you beyond a certain point—and you have to decide what that point is," he explained.

This is one of the most difficult aspects of scenario planning: deciding which risks you are going to protect against and which ones you are going to leave yourself exposed to. For example, we know that the west coast of North America is highly vulnerable to earthquakes. In fact, as with many other disasters, we know that a west coast quake, followed by a tsunami, is inevitable. We just don't know when it is going to happen.

When it happens, it won't be a surprise. And homeowners who come through it alive will also come through it financially intact because most have insurance policies that cover earthquake damage to their homes.

But if an earthquake shattered a major eastern city, most homeowners would suffer major losses because they don't have earthquake insurance. The region encompassing Ottawa, Montreal, and Quebec City is less vulnerable to quakes than the west coast but is nevertheless rated above average in vulnerability. Yet only 2 percent of Montreal homeowners have earthquake insurance, compared with 65 percent in Vancouver.

Joan McDonald, a veteran Toronto insurance broker, says that of all her hundreds of clients, only two have added earthquake protection to their home insurance polices. Torontonians seem to think they are immune from earthquakes. Yet tremors from earthquakes in the eastern U.S. have been felt in Toronto, and fault lines, albeit dormant ones, exist in and around the city. Toronto is at low risk, but not at no risk—experts do not rule out the possibility of a major quake there.

The low rate of earthquake insurance is surprising, given the dramatic rise in house prices. In parts of Toronto, some houses are worth three times their value of only a few years ago. As a result, thousands of people are now wealthy—on paper. Their wealth is contained in the deed to their house. While it is true that much of that value is in the land, which would still be there, it is also true that few homeowners have the ready cash on hand to rebuild their homes from scratch.

Are these homeowners managing their risk adequately? Not if we are to follow the example of Robert Rubin. He was prepared to take steps to protect his company against the minuscule chance of Uncle Sam defaulting on some bonds, a possibility more remote than an earthquake in eastern North America. Homeowners without earthquake coverage have decided to self-insure against that possibility— that is, assume the risk themselves.

That may well be the best decision. Perhaps these homeowners have considered the various scenarios and decided that, while the possibility of a severe earthquake is real, it is also small enough that they can justify a decision to dispense with insurance. They may also have calculated that the government would pick up some of the repair tab in the case of so major a catastrophe.

On the other hand, they may not have thought about it at all, simply because it hasn't happened yet. In that case, they are making a major financial decision blindly. Scenario planning is all about deciding consciously both to protect against certain risks and not to protect against others. It is hard to believe that 98 percent of Montreal homeowners would, had they thought about it, decide against earthquake insurance.

No one financial decision, whether to invest in India or self-insure against earthquakes, is right for each person; each person will have a different amount of regret should the decision not work out well. As we shall see in the next chapter, understanding regret, the emotional side of investing, is an essential part of effective risk management.

THE BOTTOM LINE

Proof that it is impossible to predict the future is that the most brilliant people in the world, the likes of Albert Einstein and Alexander Graham Bell, made wrong forecasts. A better way to assess the future of our investments is to consider a variety of possible futures. Then we can decide which futures to protect ourselves against and which to bet against.

The investor who is comfortable following the herd doesn't need scenarios. The investor who wants to consider all possible futures—including ones that look starkly different from the present—is by definition a scenario thinker.

There is no right scenario which is why we need sets of scenarios spanning a wide range of possible futures. A scenario set gives us a sense of the upside and downside for a particular investment. Assembling scenarios forces us to think, a useful habit for any investor.

The challenge in devising scenarios is to know how far to go on both the upside and the downside. This is important because if a downside that we deem probable would hurt us a lot, we need to revise our portfolio to protect against that eventuality.

Proxies are useful tools in creating scenarios. We don't assume that the a stock we are considering will behave exactly as a similar stock did in the past. But the history of the similar stock is one among several scenarios worth considering.

It is important to establish a worst-case scenario for each investment because that helps us decide how much money to invest, thereby placing a limit on our potential loss. If our worst-case scenario doesn't show a loss, then we need a worse worst-case scenario.

Scenarios help us anticipate surprises, such as a major earthquake in Montreal or Toronto. We may or may not decide to protect against a possible but unlikely event but it is better to make that decision consciously rather than blindly.

four

ANTICIPATE REGRET

SUPPOSE THAT you play the same numbers in a lottery every week. But one week, on an impulse, you change one of the numbers.

From a purely rational point of view, there is no problem with doing this. A lottery offers a huge upside and, as long as you gamble only small amounts, a small downside. Your chances of winning the jackpot are minuscule, and changing your numbers neither enhances nor reduces them. The odds remain the same.

From a personal perspective, however, something important changed when you decided to experiment with a different number—you drastically increased the amount of regret to which you were exposed. If that week your regular numbers won, your regret would be devastating. (Of course, if the new set of numbers you had been considering won the jackpot and you had not switched, you would also suffer regret, but less than if a set you had been playing for years won immediately after you abandoned it.)

Every investment decision is a trade-off between upside and downside. There is no upside in changing your lottery numbers, and massive downside because of the potential regret. Therefore, you should not do it.

While this example is a trivial one, potential regret is an important factor in all your financial decisions, including the biggest ones. The lottery ticket example illustrates the importance of regret especially well because one set of numbers, in terms of the odds of winning, is identical to any other. Yet in your individual case, one of them is a much worse investment than the other because of the distress it exposes you to.

Regret and downside are the same, except that regret includes emotion. If we were without emotion, there would be no downside to changing the lottery numbers. To make good investment decisions, therefore, we have to understand and anticipate regret, the emotional side of investing.

Because each individual is different, each experiences different amounts of regret when things go wrong. That is why there is no one right answer to such investment decisions as, "Should I buy Google at $300?"

The amount of regret one investor would feel if Google tumbled might be quite different from what someone else would experience. The differences are based on such factors as personality, affluence, life experience, temperament, and age. So while one person might shrug off losing $10,000 because Google went down when it was supposed to go up, another would be distraught. The actual downside—a $10,000 loss—is the same for each. But the emotion-weighted downside, regret, is quite different.

In this respect, our investment behaviour is no different from our other behaviours. Consider the case of smoking. Tobacco companies are keenly aware that few people choose to take up smoking as adults. Only young people see becoming a smoker as a positive risk-adjusted decision—that is, one in which the upside is greater than the downside. If children and teenagers did not become addicted to cigarettes, the tobacco companies could not stay in business.

Peter Jennings, the much-admired Canadian-born anchorman of ABC television news, became a cigarette smoker at the age of eleven. Joni Mitchell, the Saskatchewan-raised folk singing legend, began smoking at nine. Young people become smokers not because they have a self-destructive urge, but because, for them, the upside outweighs the downside. The upside of smoking is asserting oneself as an adult or as someone who is rebellious or cool. The downside is the likelihood of a premature death that will not occur until many decades in the future. The upside is great and is available immediately. The downside is so far away it is barely imaginable.

Peter Jennings was a compulsive smoker until he was forty-eight years old, when he quit after his first child was born. By then, he knew enough to weigh the downside of smoking more accurately. But it was too late. He died of lung cancer in August 2005, at the age of sixty-seven. Joni Mitchell, meanwhile, still smokes. She knows the downside, she explained in a *Reader's Digest* interview in 2005, but the upside—the pleasure she gets from smoking—outweighs it in her case.

Of course, millions of adults have quit the smoking habit they took up as youngsters, and many young people never start because they weigh the downside differently from those who do. A young competitive runner, for example, would avoid cigarettes in the knowledge that they would detract from her performance on the track. In each case, the individual makes what is for him a positive risk-adjusted decision.

Why do so many positive risk-adjusted decisions, like the one Peter Jennings made at age eleven when he first inhaled cigarette smoke, turn out so badly? Because people fail to consider enough scenarios or the right scenarios. And, in some cases, because their personalities lead them to be either excessive risk-takers or overly risk averse.

Anthony Richards, the thirty-two-year-old Londoner who risked his life savings on a spin of the roulette wheel, could not have acted as he did had he not weighted the downside much lower than most people would do in the same situation. Richards's upside was winning $135,000, and his downside was losing the same amount. So the risk-adjusted value was zero. If he was a rational machine instead of an irrational human being, he wouldn't have played because it was not a good bet. For a bet to be good, the upside has to be more than downside.

That's where psychology meets economics. Richards, presumably, underweighted the downside because he is a healthy, energetic thirty-two-year-old who was sure he could replace the money should the wheel not turn in his favour. It might happen that the day after he returns to London he gets into a car accident, winds up as a parapalegic, and can't replace his savings. But either he has not considered that scenario or has decided to bet against it. Because he underweights the downside, for him it is effectively less than $135,000 while the upside is $135,000. So the gamble was made in the conviction that it carried a positive risk-adjusted return.

An eighty-year-old pensioner who also had a $135,000 nest egg would not have acted the same way despite the fact his downside—$135,000—would have been identical to Richards's. For the pensioner, facing the prospect of a penniless retirement, the irreplacable $135,000 seemed like much more, whereas for Richards it seemed like much less. Just as Richards underweighted the downside, the pensioner would have overweighted it.

Because different investors ascribe different weights to the downside, we can think of regret as a multiple of the downside. The billionaires who come to frolic at the French resort of Saint-Tropez think nothing of dropping $100,000 on champagne and other stimulants over a couple of evenings. For them, the loss of $100,000 is almost nothing, because it is an insignificant portion of their wealth. The multiple of the downside of their profligate spending behaviour is a fraction of one—another way of saying that dropping $100,000 inflicts on them about as much regret as losing a two-dollar coin would cause in an average person.

Many economists have commented on the weird mental gyrations that people engage in with regard to their money. Richard Thaler, an economist at the Graduate School of Business of the University of Chicago, points out that people sometimes make strange decisions because they keep their money in different "mental accounts." A well-known example is the hypothetical case of a person who loses a $100 ticket on the way to a concert. Interviews have shown that people are less likely to buy another ticket at the box office to replace the one they lost than they are if, instead of losing a ticket, they had lost $100 in cash on the way to the concert. The reason is that $200 would be too much to spend from their entertainment account on one ticket and would inspire excessive regret. But if they lost $100 in cash, they would still be paying only $100 for a ticket, with the lost $100 being assigned mentally to their accidental-loss account rather than their entertainment account, thereby incurring less regret. Yet, regardless of what imaginary account the money had been placed in, in either case they would have spent $200 from the same actual bank account for the same evening's entertainment.

This kind of irrational thinking can be deadly to our financial health. Take the case of David, a friend of one of the authors who passed on the chance to buy stock in a technology company run by a distant relative when the stock was first issued. The stock quickly became a market sensation, soaring to (U.S.)$120. Naturally, David felt regret, and when the stock lost half its value, he jumped at the chance to make up for his initial error. He bought in, sure that a stock that was once worth $120 must now be worth a lot more than $60. He still held the stock when it reached $2.

At that point, he decided to buy another 10,000 shares.

"Is this," he was asked, "the best investment you can find for that $20,000?"

"No. There are other stocks I would rather buy."

"Then why are you buying more of this one?"

"Because I need to average down. By buying 10,000 more shares now, I bring my average cost per share way down and then, if the stock goes up, I can sell at less of a total loss."

"Averaging down" is a common stratagem of amateur investors and is sometimes even suggested by professional advisors. It involves buying more of a losing stock, not because that stock is necessarily a good investment at its current price, but to reduce the average cost of the shares, thereby reducing regret.

The same irrational thinking is at work in averaging down as in the decision not to replace a $100 ticket for a concert you really want to see, not because you can't afford the extra $100 but because the money is in the wrong mental account. David didn't buy the extra stock because he wanted more of it; he bought it so that, in his mental account, it might become a $30 stock rather than a $60 stock—and then he wouldn't suffer so much regret when he finally unloaded all of it at a loss.

It is disconcerting to realize that our so-called efficient markets are composed of the collective actions of millions of people, many of whom, like David, make senseless buy and sell decisions under the influence of regret.

This is not to say that David's decision to buy more of the technology stock was necessarily a bad move. If he had done scenario planning, he would have analyzed the company's prospects and made a decision as to whether the stock's upside, at its current price, was greater than its downside. He might have made a decision to buy, but it would have been a rational one rather than one based on emotion.

In an important sense, David's error was similar to Peter Jennings's. Both made poor decisions because they failed to assemble a sufficiently comprehensive set of scenarios from which to calculate their upsides and downsides. David made the same mistake when he bought the stock at $2 as he had when he bought it at $30—he assumed that, because it was now so much lower than it had been, it could go only up in the future.

But that was not true. It could have gone below $2 (and subsequently did), and if David had included scenarios in which that occurred he might not have bought at that price. Attempting to reduce regret is not bad in itself as long as it does not tempt us into overly optimistic scenario planning. In David's case it did. So eager was he to reduce his regret that he excluded scenarios that should have been included.

A more rational approach would have been to accept that not even the most successful investors are right every time. They understand that they will have their share of losers and, rather than try to make a loser less of a loser by averaging down, they focus on looking for the next winner.

Andrey Markov, a Russian mathematician born in 1856, probably would have been a successful stock picker. He was best known for his idea that in many situations the future develops from the present but is independent of the way in which the present developed from the past. In other words, the only thing that matters is what can happen from now on, not what happened in the past. This kind of thinking helps us weaken the grip that regret has on us so that we can make rational decisions unencumbered by emotion.

Markov would have looked at David's technology stock anew each day. He would not say, "Oh, my God, I bought this at $60 and it's now $2. Because I paid so much for it, I'm not going to sell until it gets back to $10."

Instead, he might say, "I've got something that's worth $2 on the stock market. I think it's really worth $3. I'll keep it until it hits $3 and then I'll sell." Nowhere in Markov's decision-making process would be a thought such as, "I bought it for $60, so I can't sell it until it goes up to at least $10, otherwise my loss will too horrendous."

Not making a good investment because of regret is as bad as making a bad one because of it. An example is Nortel Networks, the Canadian communications equipment manufacturer that dropped from $120 at its height in 2000 to less than $1 in 2002. Many investors, rightly, decided the stock was undervalued at less than $1 and bought it. They doubled or tripled their money without worrying about Nortel's history as a $120 stock. But someone who had bought for $100 and watched his money evaporate as the stock plunged would likely feel so much regret, he wouldn't touch the stock again, even when it had become a bargain. If these investors had adopted Markov's approach, they might have recouped some of their losses.

Benchmarks are the key factor in determining how much regret we will experience because of the performance of an investment. Perhaps I grew up in a large mansion complete with tennis court and swimming pool. Now I am living in a small apartment, which is all I can afford. It's a fine apartment—clean, modern, equipped with good appliances and the latest plasma TV—but it's not the grand house I was used to, so I am not satisfied with it and probably never will be.

But what if I grew up in an overcrowded, rat-infested slum that lacked even the most basic amenities such as running water? I would consider the same small apartment heaven on earth. It's the same place, but it's satisfactory to one person and unsatisfactory to another simply because each has a different benchmark with which to measure satisfaction.

The same phenomenon occurs in investing. David's benchmark for his $2 technology stock was $60 because that was what he paid for it. Instead of clinging to an irrelevant benchmark that had receded into the realm of fantasy, he needed to establish a more realistic one, based on the company's current situation and outlook for the future—perhaps $3. That would represent a 50 percent gain over its current price. He could then sell, satisfied that he had achieved his benchmark.

However, while he needed to establish a new benchmark for the new block of stock he had purchased, he would have been fooling himself if he had applied the new benchmark to the stock he had bought at $60. When he measures the performance of his portfolio, he needs to be honest with himself. If the stock goes to $3 and he sells it, he will still be taking a $57-per-share loss on the original shares.

Setting a benchmark too high can lead the investor to expose himself to excessive risk; at the same time, setting it too low can lead to poor investments that deliver inadequate returns. Suppose I am sixty years old, have $200,000 in my RRSP, and decide that in ten years I want to have $1 million. I am setting the benchmark extremely high. In order to reach my benchmark, I need to seek very high returns, thereby exposing myself to a lot of risk for someone of my age. The only investments that can achieve my goals are volatile ones that might be going through a down phase when it comes time to start drawing on my retirement account.

A more reasonable approach for a sixty-year-old would be to take the amount he would earn on a safe, interest-bearing investment as a benchmark. Then, if he invested part of his RRSP more aggressively in stocks and exchange-traded funds (ETFs), and exceeded the benchmark for his overall portfolio, he would be happy instead of regretful.

The benchmark you choose determines your downside. Suppose my benchmark is a 15-percent return. I will then choose only investments that have a rate of return higher than 15 percent. For me, anything less than 15 percent has only downside. In an era of low interest rates, I am going to have an ultra-risky investment portfolio.

At the other extreme, too many average investors are satisfied with consistent below-average returns. Millions of Canadians have been brainwashed to believe that managed mutual funds are the only safe way for the ordinary person to invest. They are the ones invested in funds that, because of their inflated management fees, consistently underperform the market as a whole.

People with low benchmarks will often excuse an underperforming investment with the words, "Well, at least I didn't lose money," but they are usually fooling themselves. If the investor has a mutual fund, the benchmark should be what he could have earned in a risk-free alternative—about 3 percent, the interest rate on a short-term government bond. So at the end of the year, if I haven't made more than 3 percent, then I am down.

Suppose you had bought oil at the peak of the last

bubble in 1980, when it was $38 a barrel. You then watched it dip to just above $10 in 1998 before soaring to $63 in August 2005. Now you think you've done well. But you've set your benchmark too low. The oil price would have to touch $90 to reach the inflation-adjusted high set in 1980. You would have been better off in a risk-free government bond.

For any investment, the lowest benchmark you should consider is the future value if you had put the money in a risk-free security. So if you are buying Google and planning to hold it for ten years, you could compare it to a ten-year zero-coupon bond that would cost 67 cents in 2005 for each dollar you will get at maturity. That tells you that if Google doesn't double over ten years, you will have incurred a loss in the sense that you have underperformed your benchmark.

Most people think about risk in terms of probabilities. But probability is a way of analyzing events that occur many times. Most business decisions, and many personal investment decisions, are one-time events. Thinking about probability doesn't help much with those decisions. Thinking about regret does.

Regret is sensitive to specific circumstances. To use another lottery example, imagine one that pays out only one prize, worth $1 million, and for which the tickets cost $1. All lotteries are poor investments, but this one is worse than most because there are no secondary prizes. It's all or nothing. Yet, even knowing it's almost certainly money down the drain, many people will enter because the regret—one measly dollar—is so small.

Now imagine a lottery in which the ticket costs $10,000 but the prize is $1 billion. Most buyers of the $1 tickets for the previous lottery won't consider this one, for the obvious reason that losing $10,000 would provoke major regret. But a smaller group might decide this lottery is a better play than the other because the odds of winning are better and the prize is fabulous. For them, $10,000 is merely the price of a first-class air ticket to Europe, and the regret provoked by losing it would not be excessive.

Many entrepreneurs mortgage their homes to raise money for their businesses. Others do the same to make personal investments. The upside of this action, obviously, is extracting the equity in the home and using it to create greater wealth than would have been possible otherwise. The downside is that your business or investment goes south and you lose the house. That's where individual regret comes in. Some people would take it in their stride and bounce back quickly. For others, it might be a tragedy from which they would never recover.

In building Algorithmics into a major international software company, Ron Dembo managed regret carefully. The company was funded out of its cash flow. It had neither debt nor venture capital. So as the company grew from a one-man operation in a small walk-up office to the world leader in risk management—doing business in thirty-one countries with offices in fifteen—Dembo always kept enough cash in the bank to cover salaries for six months.

In an interview with *Fast Company* magazine, Dembo described the importance of anticipating regret: "That cushion came in handy. In the early days, we had one big client, a major commercial bank, that liked our approach and helped us to fund product development. About 80 percent of our revenue came from this bank. But I kept our head count low enough to ensure that if this client dropped dead, we could survive for another six months, using that time to find new clients.

"One day, the bank changed its mind about what it wanted to do with us. It insisted that we make major revisions to our business model. Its executives thought that because they represented 80 percent of our revenue, we would do as they asked. But because we had managed our risk, we didn't need them as badly as they thought we did. So we parted ways."

The bank predicted that Algorithmics would go out of business, but instead it went on to become the world's largest risk-management software company.

"It all comes back to regret," says Dembo. "I manage regret to make sure that if something big goes wrong, I'm still covered."

Many successful entrepreneurs would have followed the same course as Dembo, anticipating regret and preparing for it. But others would have been willing to accede to the bank's demands because they might not have felt the same regret at having their freedom of action restricted. Still others, perhaps because they had never experienced setbacks, would have been totally focused on the upside and unwilling to keep in reserve large amounts of money that could be used instead to expand a growing business.

Dembo acknowledges that his course of action was a highly conservative one. The regret he anticipated was losing the company. "What does six months of capital in the bank mean? It means there is a scenario that I am considering where all my current customers stop paying, I don't sign any new orders for six months, and I want to be able to pay everybody's salary. That's a pretty negative scenario. And that's my regret. To cover my regret I put in place a big cushion."

Not everyone would have done that. Suppose Bill Gates had started up Algorithmics when he was already successful with Microsoft. If it failed, he would either pump more money into it or let it go.

Either way, he wouldn't much care, whereas Ron Dembo didn't have more money to pump into it and didn't want to lose the business and cared a lot.

What Dembo did was simply follow the old common-sense adage, "Put money aside for a rainy day." A rainy day is another term for a bad scenario. Putting money aside for it is covering your potential regret.

"Before I put in place the six-month rule, there was a scenario under which I could lose everything. Even though it was unlikely, I could be completely out of business and lose everything I've ever worked for. After I put the rule in place, only a catastrophic and extremely rare event could cause me to lose it.

"By setting aside that money, I buy the downside. My regret is now lower and my upside remains high. Now my investment is positive risk adjusted."

Many people are not able to visualize downside because they have never experienced it. The English gambler Anthony Richards would be in that category. So would the key players of Long Term Capital Management, the hedge fund described in Chapter 2.

An individual who suffers from hubris—arrogance arising from overbearing pride—will inevitably be a forecast thinker rather than a scenario thinker. He has one single forecast: that his decisions are right and always lead to upside.

How else to explain the behaviour of Dennis Kozlowski, chief executive of Tyco International, a U.S. manufacturing conglomerate, who gained notoriety for spending $2 million of the publicly traded company's money on a birthday party in Sardinia for his wife—as well as $500,000 for hand-painted wallpaper and $15,000 for an umbrella stand in his New York apartment? It apparently never occurred to him that there was a downside to such expenditures— namely that the shareholders of the company would object and he would find himself in court having to explain himself.

Other highly paid executives of large public companies have been caught in similar indiscretions. Perhaps some of them did think of alternate scenarios arising from their actions, but their single-minded upside view outweighed any visions they may have had of the downside. The lesson for investors is that there is always a downside, and if you can't find one when you do your scenario planning, keep looking until you do. And once you have identified a worst-case scenario, think of how you are going to limit your losses should that scenario actually come to pass.

When we impose on ourselves the discipline of anticipating regret we are less likely to take thoughtless risks. The risks we take become calculated risks, and those are the kind least likely to cause grief.

Suppose you are considering buying a house. Both buying and not buying entail certain risks. What to do? Simply ask yourself which decision could cause you the most regret. This is always a powerful question, because it forces you to make an objective assessment of your own personal situation, including your financial situation, your goals, and your tolerance for risk.

The upside of buying a house is obvious: you've got a place to live that you can call your own. You don't need anybody's permission to paint the living room bright yellow or rip out the back lawn and replace it with strawberry plants. And the house may increase in value, thereby becoming a good investment as well as a good place to live.

The downside is that when something goes wrong, it's your responsibility and not the landlord's. Moreover, the cost of servicing the mortgage may be more than the cost of renting, so you would have less disposable income than if you rented. Finally, there is no guarantee that the house will appreciate in value. It might go down.

To buy or not to buy? In this case, as in most investment decisions, no one answer applies to all individuals. The issue is whether the upside (your individual upside) outweighs the downside. You may have good reason to expect the value of this particular house to remain flat or even decline. That's the downside, and it's a big one. Yet this might be just the house for your needs, and it may be located in a neighbourhood that you especially like. That's a big upside.

If you buy the house, you will experience regret if you turn out to be right and it decreases in value. But you will also experience regret if you don't buy, because it was the house you really wanted. So the issue is not whether or not there will be regret, but which decision will lead to the most regret.

The decision that causes the most regret is the riskiest decision. Yet it might also be the one that carries the largest upside. You may believe the house is overpriced and that it may go down in value, but the benefits of owning that particular house are so great that, for you, the upside outweighs the downside.

You need to ask, "If I buy this house, what would I gain compared to what I would have gained had I decided to buy another house or to rent?" There may well be advantages to House B that you haven't fully considered because you are so strongly attracted to House A.

The important thing, in managing such a decision, is first to establish that the potential regret is not at an unacceptable level. The regret must not be so serious that it would adversely affect your life in a major way. What would happen, for example, if housing prices dropped by 25 percent? Would that leave you with debt greater than the value of the house? Such a situation could lead to bankruptcy. The potential regret would be too much and, should you determine that such a drop is a scenario you don't want to bet against, you would be better advised to look at a different solution to your housing needs.

It can be difficult to decide which of two or more possible decisions might lead to the most regret, because regret is often difficult to quantify. One way to put a number on it is to imagine yourself as an insurance company with an obligation to insure the downside. You might wish that you could buy an insurance policy that would pay off if your house went down in value. So if you paid $400,000 for the house and, a year later, its market value had declined to $350,000, the insurance company would pay you $50,000.

Because no such insurance policy is available, you have to self-insure your investment in the house. You are the insurance company, and you have to pay off if the house drops in value. How much value are you prepared to self-insure? $50,000? $100,000? In this context, regret can be defined as the amount of self-insurance you can tolerate. If, say, a loss of $50,000 is one of your scenarios and it would cause you intolerable distress and threaten your financial security, you should not buy.

As the reader can see, anticipating regret is a way of getting into the habit of forward thinking, the essence of what this book is about. It's about analyzing future upside and future downside and looking for investments in which subtracting downside from upside—that is, calculating the risk-adjusted upside, results in a positive number.

Too many investors make decisions on the basis of upside alone. This is dangerous because no guarantee exists that positive past results will be repeated in the future. Housing prices are a good example. Between 1975 and 1995, according to the Canada Mortgage and Housing Corporation, the average selling price of a house in Canada rose from $35,500 to $150,328. That's a dramatic increase, and it might lead one to believe that you can't go wrong buying a house. Yet in Toronto, prices dropped by 25 percent from 1989 to 1991, and some neighbourhoods did not regain their 1989 heights until the end of the 1990s. Many buyers suffered major financial setbacks because they bought at the peak and had to sell, for one reason or another, into a depressed market.

True enough, the long-term trend in house prices has been upwards. But trends don't last forever. Population growth in Canada has slowed because Canada, like the rest of the world, has declining fertility. Slower population growth means reduced demand for housing. The baby boomers, who make up about a third of the Canadian population, will begin reaching the retirement age of sixty-five in 2012. Many will retire before then. Some will decide to move from large family homes to smaller condominiums; in fact, many have already done so following the departure of their grown-up offspring from the family home. A steady flow of homes coming on the market as the huge twenty-year wave of baby boomers approaches retirement could put downward pressure on prices.

Few prospective buyers in the spring of 2005 were considering the possibility that house prices could go down. Why would they when, in the euphoric housing markets of Toronto and other major North American cities, houses were routinely selling for more than the asking price? Only a few lonely contrarians warned that, just maybe, the housing market was a bubble—and bubbles always burst. A bubble is what happens when the price of something is based more on speculation than on what the thing is actually worth. Daniel Kadlec, writing in *Time* magazine, offered this definition of a housing bubble: "We are in one when most homeowners could not afford their house at its current market value."

The most prominent doomsayer was John Talbott, a former investment banker for Goldman

Sachs, visiting scholar at the University of California at Los Angeles and the author of a 2003 book called *The Coming Crash of the Housing Market.* "The entire housing market is corrupted," Talbott wrote in the *Financial Times.* "Buyers are indifferent about how high a price they pay as it is not their money."

Many of these buyers have mortgages with floating rates. When the rates rise, as Talbott believes they will, these borrowers will not be able to make their payments. And with costlier mortgages, new buyers will not be able to qualify for large enough loans to sustain high prices. The result will be a bursting of the housing bubble in most of the developed world and a devastating crash in prices.

Talbott writes: "Just as stock brokers used to churn and burn your investment portfolio in order to generate greater commissions . . . the real estate and mortgage industry only makes money if [it] can convince you to sell, move, refinance, buy something bigger or buy a second home for vacations.

"And so we have all the elements of a traditional Ponzi scheme—assets being passed faster and faster from person to person at ever increasing 'values' in a furious game in which the only person who loses is the last one out."

When a trend, such as rising house prices, is well established and powerful, we are always tempted to assume it will continue. We do not seek out a set of scenarios, but rather cling to one forecast: that the future will be an extrapolation of the present. Basing a major decision such as a house purchase on one single forecast is dangerous. The government of China could, should it choose to, put a stop to rising house prices in North America. The United States finances its huge budget deficit by borrowing from foreign creditors such as the Bank of China, which has been accumulating about $200 billion worth of U.S. debt a year. If it decided to accumulate less, the United States would have to raise its interest rates to get new investors to finance its deficit. In that case, Canadian interest rates would likely also rise. A 2-percent rise in the interest rate would translate into $8,000 a year in extra payments on a $400,000 mortgage. If that happened, some people wouldn't be able to pay. They would have to put their houses on the market. And fewer new buyers would be able to afford the going rate for houses. House prices would stop rising and start dropping.

That's one scenario. Another is that, rather than a crash, we will instead see moderate decreases or a period of price stability. People do need places to live and, while population growth is slower than in the past, births continue to outnumber deaths in Canada and so the population continues to grow. Builders will react to declining demand by slowing the pace of new construction, thereby reducing the supply of new housing and bolstering the price of existing homes. Many retired boomers will stay in their large empty nests where they can create home offices for themselves and guest rooms for visiting children and grandchildren. These houses may not come on the market for several decades when their boomer occupants move into nursing homes or die. And new immigrants will continue to arrive in Canada, adding to population growth and therefore to the demand for housing.

We can't know for certain what will happen to housing prices in the years ahead. The best we can do, in an uncertain world, is to consider all the possibilities and account for risk before making our decision. The good news is that such an approach increases our chances of success. When you consider all possible futures, including the scary one proposed by Talbott, you are less likely to make irrational moves. You won't get caught up in the euphoria of a financial bubble and you will protect yourself from unacceptable levels of regret.

The bad news is that even if our forward-looking approach leads us to the right decision, success is not guaranteed. To illustrate the point, suppose you buy the safest car on the market and keep it well maintained. You always wear your seat belts and drive cautiously. Then, one day, while you are stopped at a red light, an out-of-control truck smashes into you.

You did everything right but you still got killed.

In another scenario, you never wear your seat belt, your car's brakes need replacing, and you never get the car serviced. One day, you are travelling at high speed, and have to slam on the brakes quickly; they fail, and you get killed.

It's important to understand that these two cases are not the same. In the first case, you did the best you possibly could and you were unlucky in an uncertain world. In the second, you engaged in highly risky behaviour and suffered the consequences.

We can never eliminate risk. All we can do is manage it, by making sure the brakes on our investment portfolio have been checked and the seat belts fastened. In the next chapter we will look at how to do that.

THE BOTTOM LINE

Two investors each lose $10,000 on the same investment. The first, being wealthier, shrugs it off while the other is grief-stricken. Because of regret, the downside for the second investor is greater than that of the first. Regret is the emotion-weighted downside.

Regret can lead to irrational investment decisions. One of the most common is "averaging down" in which investors buy more of a losing stock for the sole reason of reducing the average loss per share, thereby also reducing regret.

To make rational investment decisions it is best to look forward rather than backward. If Nortel is selling for $1, the issue is whether it is a good investment at that price, not that you lost money on it previously when its share price collapsed.

Benchmarks determine how much regret we will experience. It is important that we set realistic benchmarks. Setting a bench-mark too high can leave the investor exposed to excessive risk. Setting it too low can result in unacceptably low returns.

Anticipating regret makes us less likely to make poor decisions. We still take risks but they are calculated risks rather than thoughtless ones.

five

STRATEGIES *for the* RISK-AWARE INVESTOR

BY NOW, when you think of your investment portfolio you will:

- · Know what you own
- · Use multiple scenarios to analyze your upside and downside
- · Anticipate your regret

You understand the scenarios that hurt you and those that make you money. You know whether any probable scenario could have a severe impact on your wealth. You know you are protecting yourself against certain scenarios—and consciously leaving yourself unprotected against others because you have deemed them improbable. You understand whether your portfolio, on a risk-adjusted basis, is worth keeping— that is, whether its upside is bigger than its downside.

So, what do you do if a scenario presents itself that could destroy more value than you care to risk in your portfolio? What do you do if you have previously neglected to consider a scenario and now want to include it? What do you do if you discover that, because of changing circumstances, your upside is now less than your downside? What do you do if the regret under a scenario that you have considered is too high? These are some of the questions we will try to answer in this chapter.

Let's assume one of your scenarios is a near-doubling in interest rates from 4 percent currently to 7 percent in one year from now. You consider this an unlikely event, but your financial advisor insists that you protect yourself against it because you are heavily invested in bonds and income trusts that will plummet in value if the scenario materializes.

The solution is simple: you buy insurance. How does one go about insuring a portfolio against a scenario in which the interest rate rises from 4 percent to 7 percent or higher? There are several strategies, some easier to implement than others. The simplest would be to focus on the part of the portfolio that is most vulnerable under this scenario and reduce it by enough that, even if the rate spiked to 10 percent, the loss would be bearable. That would mean dumping some of the portfolio's bond and income trust holdings.

Alternatively, the investor could buy some other securities whose values go up when interest rates go up, thereby at least partly offsetting the loss. For example, the investor could increase the amount of money he has in short-term deposits such as money market funds. If the rates rise, so will the income these securities earn. After the rates have risen, he will have other options for the use of this money, such as lending some of it out as a mortgage. Once these changes have been made, the investor needs to analyze the revamped portfolio under all the original scenarios and begin the process of risk management over again.

Finally, the investor may consider buying derivatives to insure his portfolio directly against the impact of the feared rate rise. This strategy is simpler and, because the transaction costs are lower, cheaper to implement than revamping the holdings in a portfolio. As explained in Chapter 1, a derivative is a financial instrument whose value depends on the performance of an underlying security or asset. Trading in derivatives by people who do not own the underlying securities is a form of high-stakes gambling. In 1995, a trader named Nick Leeson, by making huge bets using derivatives, destroyed Barings Bank, one of Britain's oldest financial institutions. Such incidents led Warren Buffett, the legendary investment genius, to label derivatives "weapons of mass destruction."

But derivatives can also be used by the most cautious of investors to protect their portfolios against undesirable future events. This is done by combining a derivative that moves in one direction with an underlying security that moves in the opposite direction. Think of the insurance policy on your house. It is a piece of paper that rises in value when, because of a fire or some other calamity, your house declines in value. Derivatives are the same: pieces of paper that rise in value when something bad happens to an underlying security. Just as with house or car insurance, sometimes no perfect match exists between the available policies and our exact need. Fortunately, the derivatives market is growing quickly and delivering new products to insure almost any kind of financial risk. Not all of these products are available for the ordinary investor, but more are becoming available daily. Investors should seek out expert advice to help in choosing the appropriate derivatives to insure their portfolios.

The derivatives we use for insuring against such events as a rise in interest rates or a decline in a certain stock—or the stock market as a whole—are known as *options*. These give us the right to buy or sell a security at a set price for a set period of time. A "call option" gives us the right to buy, while a "put option" gives us the right to sell. In this case, we want to insure against interest rates rising above 7 percent in one year's time, so the derivatives we buy will be based on some underlying rate-sensitive security such as a government treasury bill. If interest rates rise above 7 percent we want to be paid one dollar for every one-dollar drop in our portfolio. Because a 7-percent interest rate is a long shot, this particular interest-rate option will be cheap.

The option will pay its owner in all situations where interest rates are above 7 percent in a year's time. The more the rate rises above 7 percent, the more it will pay. So, by buying an appropriate amount of calls, the investor is compensated for his portfolio's losses.

The more volatile interest rates are, the higher the price of the calls. Closeness of the "strike price" (the price at which the option is exercised) to the actual rate also raises the price of the call. Both of these variables increase the likelihood that the event being insured against will actually happen, so it is not surprising that the insurance would cost more.

In the way it is priced, portfolio insurance is comparable to home insurance. It will be cheaper to insure your Montreal house against damage from earthquakes the day before a major earthquake occurs than the day after. Similarly, the cost of insuring your portfolio against a rise in the interest rate increases with the volatility of the interest-rate market.

Just as your home-insurance policy is worthless the day after its expiry date, so are your interest-rate calls. If you had known in advance that rates would not exceed 7 percent, you could have saved yourself some money by not buying them. But of course we don't know what will happen in the future, so it makes good sense to insure some of our downside.

Call options insure against losses caused when a financial security rises in value. Put options, in contrast, insure against the impact of something dropping in value. Suppose you have a large amount of money invested in the stock of one of the major banks. You figure this is a good long-term investment but, because of some odd strategic moves by the bank and turmoil in the executive suite, you are worried about the next six months. You own 1,000 shares, so you decide to buy 1,000 puts. Your shares are currently valued at $50, and the puts give you the right to sell 1,000 shares at $40 (the strike price) for the next six months. If the stock stays above $40, your puts aren't worth anything. But if it suddenly dives to $25, they are worth $15 each. By buying the puts, you have insured yourself against part of the loss you would incur if this important part of your investment portfolio suffered a severe setback.

The investor can also insure against a downward slide in a particular stock market as a whole. Suppose she owns an exchange-traded fund (ETF) that is equivalent to the S&P 500 index of large-capitalization U.S. stocks. She buys a put option on the S&P 500 that will pay, at maturity, a certain amount for every point below the option's strike price. By buying enough of these options, the investor protects herself against a costly downturn in the U.S. stock market.

In Chapter 2, we singled out ignorance as the most dangerous of all the risks that affect one's financial well-being. Just as it is essential that investors understand the way the financial services industry works and the nature of various financial instruments that comprise their portfolios, so it is important, if we wish to manage risk successfully, to understand how portfolio insurance works. Many excellent guide books are available on options and their uses. A good place to start are the booklets put out by the Chicago and Montreal option exchanges.

A vast array of options is available, and the choice

grows daily. Today's investor can insure (or "hedge," as the experts would say) anything from the weather to the price of oil to exotic currencies. We believe that options are on the verge of being discovered by the broad investing public. Mutual funds existed for decades before becoming the chosen investment instrument of average investors during the 1980s. Similarly, options have a long history, but only a minority of investors have understood and used them.

Options are too useful a risk-management tool to remain the preserve of a relatively small group of financial sophisticates. This is an area where advisors can play a vital role. Anyone who calls himself a financial advisor should have an expert understanding of options and be able to guide his clients in how to use them to insure the downside of their investment portfolios. In this way, investment advisors can make risk more manageable for the average investor than ever before.

Scenarios are never cast in stone, because the world changes every hour of every day. Occasionally, a major event occurs that dramatically alters our scenarios. Suppose, for example, that on September 10, 2001, you used scenario analysis to set up a portfolio with a positive risk-adjusted value. The next day, a terrorist attack on the U.S. occurred that not only played havoc with stock markets but invalidated all existing scenario sets. Post–September 11, the probability of large-scale terrorist attacks on urban populations had to be included in all scenario planning. So, risk conscious investors had to re-examine their scenarios.

The new scenarios you develop in such an environment affect the values of the upside and downside and could cause you to rethink your investment strategy. But it is important to avoid too narrow a focus on the recent past, thereby skewing scenario choices to a short-term view. A better approach is to keep your old scenarios and add some new ones reflecting recent events. Your original scenarios are still valid descriptions of what the future might hold. What has changed is that their likelihood of occurring is reduced because they do not account for the probability of future attacks.

One doesn't remake one's portfolio because of every world event. Only significant events require major surgery. These might be bad events such as a war, a nuclear accident, or a global flu epidemic. Or they might be good events, such as a technological breakthrough that slashes energy costs, a vaccine for AIDS, an economic resurgence in Germany and Japan, or a peace treaty in the Middle East. Each major event should cause us to reflect on the choices we have made and to test them against the realities of the changed world. Even in the absence of a major event, many small events will add up to enough change over the passage of time to require a re-examination of our scenarios, portfolio makeup, and risk-management strategy. This should be done at least once a year.

What do you do if, after analyzing your portfolio in light of a new scenario set, you discover that its upside is less than its downside? The answer to this question depends on the individual. Because we live in an uncertain world, even a negative-risk-adjusted portfolio can turn out to be profitable. For this reason, the more risk-tolerant investor may decide to bet against the odds and keep his risky portfolio intact.

Others will want to make adjustments that improve the upside, reduce the downside, or do both simultaneously. Perhaps the problem involves a single stock. You could buy puts on the stock, as described above. This strategy adjusts the downside with a small cost to the upside. Or you could simply dump the stock.

The most important thing is to get into the habit of using risk-adjusted value as your measure. Again, this means that we analyze the upside and downside using a realistic and comprehensive scenario set and determine that the upside outweighs the downside. The advantage of this system is that it is forward looking. This means that you disregard any past history you may have had with a particular stock or fund and view the investment objectively going forward. You don't throw out history altogether, because your scenarios incorporate information from that past that helps you frame the various possible futures. Using knowledge about the past is sensible. What is not sensible is clinging to a stock, or buying more of it to "average down," just because in the past you bought it for a given price and cannot tolerate the regret of dumping it.

One way you can fix the upside is to look for investments to add to your portfolio that will increase its upside while not affecting the downside—or, even better, reducing the downside. An expert equipped with "optimization" software can help. This software scans the market for the investments your particular portfolio needs. A truly professional advisor will have such tools or will have ready access to them.

A financial advisor should be much more than a salesperson of mutual funds whose only information is the latest forecasts from the propaganda machine of a mutual fund company. Is your advisor a true professional or just a salesperson? Here are some questions to ask that will help you find out:

· Can you tell me the risk factors that affect my portfolio?
· Can you advise me on scenarios that I should be considering when evaluating my existing portfolio or your suggestions for additions to it?
· Given my portfolio and your suggested changes, can you tell me what my new upside/downside is with the changes included?

Advisors who can't provide convincing answers to these questions aren't providing real investment advice. They are simply throwing darts at a board. Often they are paid for every dart they throw on your behalf. In such cases, the dart-throwing benefits the advisor more than the investor.

If advisors are to become true professionals, investors need to stop thinking of financial advice as something that comes for free. If the advisor's only source of income is fees from mutual fund companies, then he is working for the mutual fund companies, not for the investor. He is going to sell the high-fee mutual funds that allow him to earn a living, not exchange-traded funds or options whose "manufacturers" do not pay fees to salespersons.

If the investor is paying his advisor, either on a

fee-for-service basis or through a percentage of assets invested, then the advisor will be working for the investor. In exchange, the investor will have every right to expect the advisor to have a thorough understanding of financial risk and of the increasingly sophisticated tools available to manage it. A role will always exist for advisors, but that role should be more transparent and should add more value.

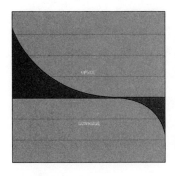 

INVESTMENT A   INVESTMENT B

Figure 1.

Look at the two drawings in Figure I. Let's call them Investment A and Investment B. The bottom part is the downside and the top part is the upside. The two graphs could represent any kind of comparable investment. Investment A might be a house in a prosperous real estate market with a growing population, while Investment B is a house in a less stable market with a weak economy. Or perhaps they are a pair of mutual funds: A is a no-load dividend fund, composed of dividend-paying blue chip Canadian stocks. It has a low management expense ratio and consistently out-performs its benchmark index; B is a fund composed of stocks of companies in the emerging markets. While capable of occasionally delivering high returns, it is volatile, exposes Canadian investors to currency risk, and is burdened with a high management-expense ratio.

All investments carry risk, but in this comparison it is clear that, in both these examples, Investment A carries less risk than Investment B. As depicted in Figure 1, A, for every dollar of potential downside has $5 of upside. B, for every dollar of potential downside has only 50 cents of upside. That is another way of saying that the *cost of capital* is less for Fund A—with capital defined as the value that would be lost under the worst-case scenario.

Suppose you were to invest the same amount in both and receive the same return from both—say, 10 percent. It is important to understand that those returns are not equal. You exposed yourself to more risk when you put money into Fund B than when you invested in Fund A. So while a 10-percent return from the dividend fund is satisfactory given that your principal was relatively safe, the same return from the emerging-markets fund is not acceptable. On a risk-adjusted basis, it is significantly less than your return from the dividend fund.

This concept becomes clearer if we think of each investment we make as a business, which in fact it is. When we buy shares of a company or units of a mutual fund, we become the part owner of a business or businesses from which we expect to earn money. The riskier our business, the greater our chance both of large profits and of large losses. Venture capitalists who invest in small start-up businesses understand the concept of risk-adjusted return very well. Because most start-ups fail, they lose money on most of their investments. That's why they demand huge returns from the few that succeed.

Perhaps our investment actually is an operating business. Let's assume that Investment A is a franchise in a well-established restaurant chain that has steady growth in same-store sales and a minuscule closure rate, while Investment B is a franchise in a newer, unproven restaurant chain with a high closure rate. Any business has to have money in the bank to cover various expenses, including unexpected surprises. But the owner of Franchise B needs more money in the bank than the owner of Franchise A because more things could go wrong for Franchise B. The owner of Franchise A, because it is well known and established, has thousands of loyal customers before he opens his doors. Franchise B is less well known and so won't have the same amount of business in the early months. Therefore, the franchisee will need more capital to keep this business afloat until revenues increase enough to put him in the black.

The riskier the investment, the more capital it requires. This is as true of an investment in a financial instrument such as a stock or a mutual fund as it is of an investment in an operating business such as a rental property or a restaurant. You may not actually invest more money in Risky Fund B than in Conservative Fund A, but because B has a greater downside, more of your capital is at risk. If there are more chances that you could lose, you need more capital to support the business (in this case, the business being your investment in Fund B) because in bad times you are going to have to pay out.

Does this mean you should not put any money into B? Not necessarily. Assume that the two graphs represent two different index funds, each analyzed according to the same set of scenarios. For Index Fund A, there are a lot of scenarios where you make money and only a few where you lose money. For Index Fund B, the situation is reversed: there are only a few scenarios where you win and a lot where you lose. In other words, these two funds perform differently under the same scenarios.

So why would you want to put any money in B? Because unexpected things happen. Maybe A will plunge in value if a SARS epidemic sweeps across North America or an earthquake levels Los Angeles, while those same disasters might make B a winner. Odd as it may seem to consider a risky investment as insurance, the high-downside Fund B might be just what you need to insure your larger holdings in low-downside Fund A. This is similar to buying an option to insure a stock that we own. Buying the option on its own is a risky gamble. Buying it because it moves in the opposite direction from a stock we own is insurance.

But since Fund A is a better bet, it makes sense to have a bigger investment in A than in B. This is true even if B was up 30 percent last year while A was down. If Fund A has more positive scenarios than B, it is a better bet if you are investing for the long term, regardless of its most recent performance.

You can't know how well an investment performed unless you know its risk-adjusted return. Maybe someone you know bought a house as an investment and sold it a year later for a $100,000 profit, and now he is telling you what a smart real estate speculator he is. You can't judge the degree to which this investment was a success without knowing how much risk was taken to obtain it. People are happy to talk about end results when they are good, but they are less forthcoming about the risks they took.

Maybe your friend the speculator doesn't want you to know that he had to borrow at usurious rates because he couldn't satisfy the requirements of conventional lenders. Or maybe he took the money out of his daughter's education fund. In that case, even though he made a profit, his risk-adjusted return may well have been unacceptably low because the downside—no money to send his daughter to university—was so high.

A PORTFOLIO INSURANCE STRATEGY

A basic principle of investing is to avoid losing money. Some investors, so concerned about honouring that principle, become excessively risk averse. They park all their money in no-risk investments such as government bonds and money market funds. They don't lose under that system, but they don't give themselves a chance to make much, either.

For the investor with a view to the long term, there is a better system: one that protects the initial principal amount and still allows a chance—no guarantee, but a good chance—for big gains.

Suppose you have just turned fifty-five and have $200,000 in savings and a house worth $300,000. Let's assume you plan to retire at sixty-five when you will begin to collect a pension of $5,000 a month.

Now imagine yourself at sixty-five and think of the worst-case scenario you could accept at that time. You would want, at the very least, to continue to live comfortably. Even though you hadn't succeeded in investing your money profitably, you would still have the original $200,000. In retirement, you would be able to start drawing on that nest egg for special expenses such as travel and as a supplement to your pension. If you needed more money to supplement your income, you would be able to take out a reverse mortgage on your house.

So to start, let's guarantee the $200,000. To do this, you buy a zero-coupon government bond that would have cost you, in 2005, about $130,000. A zero-coupon bond is one in which the "coupons," or regular interest payments, have been stripped away and sold separately. The buyer of the bond pays a discount to its face value that varies according to the prevailing interest rate and the amount of time to maturity. He then collects the full face value—in this case, $200,000—at maturity.

Now you have guaranteed that, at a minimum, you will have $200,000 in ten years. In other words, you have insured your principal. Yet you still have $70,000 left, money that can be invested more aggressively in search of big returns. Even in the worst-case scenario, in which you lose the $70,000 with a bad investment, you are still protected.

So, what to do with the $70,000? One simple yet effective course would be to put it into one or more exchange-traded funds (ETFs) that contain all the stocks in a particular stock market. The rationale behind buying an index is that, since most mutual funds cannot outperform the market, it is better simply to buy the whole market. The index instruments, because they do not require the services of a stock-picking manager and are not sold by fee-collecting advisors, have much lower management fees than an actively managed fund.

In Canada, the most popular ETF is the i6o, which contains the sixty largest stocks on the Toronto Stock Exchange in proportion to their market capitalization. If you decide to put the entire $70,000 into the i6o, you are placing a bet on the performance of Canada's sixty largest companies over a ten-year period. The composition of this roster of companies will change with their rising and falling fortunes, but it's a good bet that you will not lose money in this investment over a ten-year period. That worst-case scenario could happen, but only in the event of a devastating, long-term recession.

As one of your saddest downside scenarios, we could take as a proxy the experience of the Japanese stock market in its worst ten-year period. If your $70,000 had been invested before the Japanese stock bubble burst, it would have been worth $20,000 ten years later. So, even in this terrible scenario, you still have $220,000 at the end of ten years.

Much more likely is that your $70,000 will have doubled, leaving you with $340,000, or $140,000 more than you started with. This is a good risk-adjusted performance, given that your original principal amount, $200,000, was fully protected—another way of saying that your downside was zero.

A more conservative version of this strategy would be to take expected inflation into account. Depending on your estimate of future inflation, you would put more of the starting principal into the risk-free zero-coupon bond, thereby ensuring that, at the very least, you have the same amount of money, in inflation-adjusted dollars, in ten years as when you started. This strategy may err on the side of caution, however, by reducing the amount available to put into a higher-risk, higher-reward type of investment.

Another choice for the $70,000 we are investing aggressively is to put it into a hedge fund—not just any hedge fund, but one run by a stable, reputable institution. A hedge fund differs from an ETF such as the i60 in important ways. In the ETF, you know exactly what you own, the fees are minuscule, and your investment will neither outperform nor under-perform the market as a whole. In the hedge fund, you don't know what you own, the fees are high, and its performance, if it truly is a hedge fund, will have little in common with the overall market. It might outperform the market spectacularly—or it might do a lot worse.

Having criticized mutual funds for their high management fees, why would we suggest putting even a small portion of one's wealth into a hedge fund that sports even higher fees? To answer that question, consider the concepts of alpha and beta. *Beta,* in the investment business, means market return. An ETF, because it mirrors the market, is pure beta. *Alpha* rep-resents money-management skill. Most large, diversified mutual funds perform a bit better or a bit worse than their benchmark indexes. This tells us that the performance of these funds is largely based not on what the manager does, but on beta. Only a small portion of it comes from alpha. If only 10 per-cent or less of the fund's performance is due to alpha and you are paying a management fee of 2 percent, then you are being overcharged.

A hedge fund, on the other hand, makes no attempt to correlate its investments to a benchmark index. More typically, it may target a return well in excess of any index, and it does so using a variety of strategies, some of them quite complex, as described in Chapter 2. Whereas an ETF is pure beta, a hedge fund is pure alpha.

If you are going to pay high fees for anything, you should be doing it only for high-risk investments with high expected returns, managed on a basis of alpha. You can buy beta cheaply in the form of ETFs. If you overpay for beta by buying conventional managed mutual funds, the returns will be swamped by the high fees.

Hedge funds aren't as expensive when one considers that the higher the expected return, the lower the management fees are as a percentage of the return. For example, for some mutual funds the fees might constitute more than 50 percent of the expected return, while for high-return hedge funds the ratio is often less than 20 percent, even though the absolute fee percentage is the same or more.

Because the holdings of a hedge fund are so varied and change so quickly, we have to revise "know what you own" to "know *whom* you own." By investing in a hedge fund, the investor is placing a bet on its management. She needs to satisfy herself that the managers are highly skilled and that they have their own money invested in the fund they are managing.

Is investing in a hedge fund risky? Absolutely. A large part of your $70,000 could be lost. But this book is about managing risk, not about avoiding it. By investing $130,000 of your $200,000 nest egg in a zero-coupon government bond, you managed your risk by ensuring that, at the end of ten years, in your worst-case scenario, you still have $200,000.

In this investment strategy, even if the worst happens, your regret won't be excessive. And the odds are good that the worst won't happen and that you will have much more than $200,000 at the end of ten years. Put another way, your upside is greater than your downside. In investing, that's the best we can ever do.

THE BOTTOM LINE

We can insure an investment portfolio just as we insure a house or car. One way is to buy options that go up when the investment being insured goes down.

Scenarios are never static because the world changes every day. Major economic and political events require us to revise our existing scenarios or add new ones. This may in turn affect the values of our upside and downside, thereby requiring changes in our portfolio to ensure that it still has a positive risk-adjusted value.

We don't know how well an investment performed unless we know its risk-adjusted return. A very risky investment that returns a modest profit has a negative risk-adjusted return.

A good portfolio insurance strategy is to put the largest part of an initial investment into a zero-coupon bond that pays a guaranteed amount at maturity. The rest goes into a higher risk investment, such as an index or hedge fund, that has the potential to deliver high returns. The zero-coupon bond at maturity will be worth the same as the entire initial investment, so the downside is zero while the upside is large. In investing, that's as good as it gets.

ACKNOWLEDGEMENTS

The authors would like thank their diligent agent, Beverly Slopen, and enthusiastic editor, Nick Massey-Garrison. They are also indebted to Leanne Baskett who provided valuable logistical support and Matthew Chaffe who produced the diagrams. Daniel Stoffman is grateful to his in-house editor, Judy Stoffman, for her thoughtful suggestions and advice.

INDEX

faultiness of, 11, 19–20,
83–85
objectivity and, 80–81
role in creating bubbles,
113–14
why people believe
them, 78–81
why they're faulty, 76,
83–85
foreign-exchange risk, 48,
106
Friedman, Thomas, 103
front-end loads, 38

G

Gates, Bill, 80
Genentech, 77
General Electric, 127–28
General Motors, 25, 128
geopolitics, 107–8, 115,
178–80
global warming, 122–26
Globefund.com, 43
Goldman, William, 85
Goldman Sachs, 11–13,
117
Google, 90–94, 97–101

Grasset, Stephany, 31–32,
37–38
green energy, 127–30
greenhouse gases, 123–25,
131
Greenspan, Alan, 87,
95

H

hedge funds, 50–61
compared with
exchange-traded
funds, 192
compared with mutual
funds, 51–53
importance of man-
agers, 192–94
lack of transparency,
56–57, 60–61
Long Term Capital
Management
(LTCM), 53–56
management fees,
57–58
herd instinct, 84–85,
91–92, 113–14,
118–19

206 ↑ INDEX

ABOUT THE AUTHORS

DR. RON S. DEMBO is the founder and former president of Algorithmics Incorporated, and grew it from a startup to the largest enterprise risk management software company in the world, with offices in fifteen countries and over half of the world's top banks as clients. He was a professor at Yale, has published over sixty technical papers on Finance and Mathematical Optimization, and holds a number of patents in computational finance. He is the founder and CEO of zerofootprint.org. In 2003 he was among the first fifty people inducted into the Risk Hall of Fame.

DANIEL STOFFMAN is the co-author of the best-selling *Boom, Bust & Echo*. His most recent book, *Who Gets In: What's Wrong with Canada's Immigration Program and How to Fix It* was a finalist for the Donner Prize and the Shaughnessy Cohen Prize.